sculptural
metal clay
JEWELRY

sculptural
metal clay
JEWELRY

INTERWEAVE.
interweavestore.com

TECHNIQUES **+** EXPLORATIONS

KATE McKINNON

EDITOR
Jean Campbell

ART DIRECTOR
Liz Quan

COVER + INTERIOR DESIGN
Pamela Norman

STEP PHOTOGRAPHY
Joe Coca + Kate McKinnon

PROJECT PHOTOGRAPHY
Joe Hancock

STYLIST
Pam Chavez

PRODUCTION
Katherine Jackson

Interweave Press, LLC
201 East Fourth Street
Loveland, CO 80537
interweavestore.com

Printed in China by Imago.

Library of Congress Cataloging-in-Publication Data
McKinnon, Kate.
  Sculptural metal clay jewelry : techniques and
explorations / Kate McKinnon.
      p. cm.
  Includes bibliographical references and index.
  ISBN 978-1-59668-174-3 (pbk.)
 1. Jewelry making. 2. Precious metal clay. I.
Title.
  TT212.M39255 2010
  739.27—dc22
                            2009047741

10 9 8 7 6 5 4 3 2 1

contents

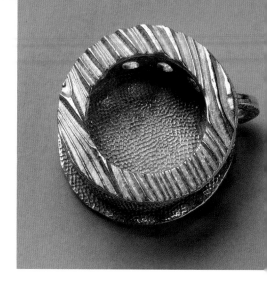

introduction

THIS BOOK IS A POEM to the possibilities of pure fine silver, which is too often overlooked by traditional metalsmiths. Fine silver is just pure silver, with nothing added or alloyed to it, and it comes in many forms. Fine silver metal clay can be textured, sculpted, hand built, or coaxed into almost any shape imaginable, and, if properly worked and fired, can be almost as dense and durable as cast metal. Pure fine silver wire or sheet can not only be joined in the flame, or fused, without using solder or flux, but can also be imbedded into metal clay work and bonded in the kiln. This allows you to bring the solid structure of pulled or rolled metal to support your sculptural metal clay pieces, forming ring shanks, posts, armatures and prong settings.

The use of pure silver, whether in clay, sheet metal, or wire form, not only eliminates the need for solder or chemicals at the bench, it offers freedom from the time-consuming (and dirty) process of cleaning and polishing back the blackening that comes from heating alloys like sterling silver. When using fine silver, I can work metal from beginning to end safely and cleanly. I can make, in just a few hours, complex and detailed finished pieces, any one of which can be used as a prototype for casting if I wish. No wax carving is necessary, and my casting models are permanent works, not burned away in the molding process.

If you've ever done any traditional metalsmithing, those two paragraphs might sound revolutionary. Most people who work metal haven't been taught that fine silver can be fused, instead of soldered, or have been told that it is too soft to make "real" jewelry with. It isn't. You just have to make things slightly more solid, or thicker in gauge. Properly handled, sized, and work-hardened, fine silver can serve beautifully, even in high-stress positions like ring bands and chain.

Although many talented artisans are working with fine silver wire and metal clay, I find that two vitally important steps in understanding and working any metal are often left out of most books and classes on metal clay: annealing and forging. For example, few metal clay artisans are aware of the true reason that a full firing is so important:

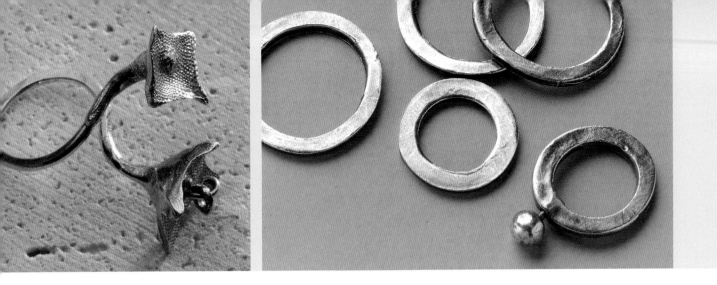

the benefit of a deep annealing soak. Even fewer are aware that they can melt their scrap, cast it into an ingot of pure silver, and then roll their own fine silver sheet or draw their own wire.

Although some of the projects presented in this book may seem complex if you are a beginner, they are just progressions of simple steps, and anyone can make them. No special equipment is required other than a set of basic clay tools, pliers, and cutters, and access to a digitally controlled kiln. Each technique and project, in addition to showing the simplest path to completion, also shows many variations. I'll encourage you to practice basic skills, no matter what your level of experience: to find body memory for your tasks, to solidify your skills, and to add a meditative quality to your work that can lead you to a well of original ideas.

A helpful section in the front of the book explains fine silver metal clay from the particles on up: what it is and why full firing, annealing, and work-hardening are so important. There's a handy glossary of terms, both for metalsmithing and for clay work, and a series of techniques and projects meant to build your skills as a craftsperson.

If you're a beginner, the enclosed DVD will give you step-by-step guidance for handling and working the clay, and if you're an experienced artisan, you might enjoy the details of the more complex projects. If your experience has been limited to working only with the clay, the sections on fine silver fusing, riveting, annealing, and forging will take your skills to the next level.

The techniques you use in your craft are your own playground, your laboratory, your teachers, your magic circle. Only when you fully inhabit them do they become your own, so give yourself to each one, and practice them until your fingers know the way.

You'll be swimming in ideas. I promise.
— **KATE McKINNON**

basics

The more I work with fine silver metal clay, the more possibilities I see, and the more interesting it becomes. I began using it in 1997, when I wanted to make my own specialty clasps and connecting elements for my beadwork. After exploring it for a year or so, I began learning traditional metalsmithing techniques so that I'd have a better understanding of my options for making cleaner connections and stronger pieces.

Fine silver metal clay is a valuable addition to any jeweler's bench, and it's not only possible, but delightful, to make finished work of professional quality in pure fine silver. Alloys like sterling silver are lovely in context and offer technical benefits in strength and durability, but in my opinion, nothing compares to the depth and beauty of pure silver. The time spent mastering the somewhat different skill sets to work with it is well worth your while.

I work with metal clay very simply and cleanly, and nothing I do is particularly complex or difficult. I don't add anything to it, and I try to move quickly and deliberately to my forms, without overhandling. My techniques for forming the clay are all classic hand-building skills, and I work with the clay differ-

ently in each of the basic stages of dryness. Throughout the book I'll point out to you which things work better in these different stages.

I encourage you to explore even the most basic tasks fully and watch the enclosed DVD to learn even more about these basic techniques. You haven't really rolled a ball of clay, for example, until you've rolled an utterly smooth, totally compressed egg of clay with just a few motions. Ideally, your work will be so neatly made that you'll never be forced to sand or file a single piece of dry or fired metal clay unless you choose to do so. Doing potentially dangerous things with any material should be a choice, not a default. In general, the less you file and sand metal clay or metal, the healthier you and your work environment will be.

What Is Metal Clay?

It's important to remember that metal clay really is metal. Even though it's in a flexible binder material and behaves much like any other type of clay, it's made up of many tiny particles of silver. It's your job to keep those particles as tightly packed together as possible, and, when firing your pieces, to give them enough heat, for enough time, for the zillions of tiny particles of metal bond to form as dense a finished piece as possible. This is why I will repeatedly encourage you to do things that compress, rather than stretch, your clay, and to fire your work fully (for 2 hours, at 1650° F [899° C]) to allow the pieces enough time in the kiln to be dense and strong enough to forge, size, and work at your bench. Many people are taught to routinely short-fire or underfire their metal clay and this is unfortunate, as it deprives them of the opportunity to work with the finished pieces like a metalsmith would.

There are various silver clay formulas on the market, each with slightly different particle sizes and binder compositions, but they all behave the same once their binder materials are burned out in the kiln. That happens rather quickly, at about 700–800° F (371–427° C). After the binder flames out, the process of *sintering* begins. Sintering is the bonding of tiny particles into a whole, in this case, using heat. Bringing your piece as close as possible to the fusing temperature of fine silver (~1700° F [927° C]) will make for denser and stronger work.

Working with Metal Clay

Metal clay is malleable and versatile, but it dries very quickly and your work time can be quite short. Your challenge is to keep your working clay fresh and moist. Rather than adding water to it, which diminishes its sculptural workability, the best way to keep it fresh is to roll the metal clay into a smooth ball with no cracks (see *Rolled Balls and Simple Shapes*, page 20) and place it in a small airtight container, where it can remain fresh and workable for months.

In general, you should handle the clay as little as possible. It dislikes being touched, pulled, rolled, and I'm reasonably sure it gets irritated if you look directly at it. With traditional clay bodies, if your clay gets too dry, a little spritz of water and a bit of time under a plastic sheet works wonders to rehydrate it. With metal clay, if you miss your moment, it may be well and truly gone.

While your piece may not be savable, if you miss your moment, there are ways to revive or repurpose your clay if it

---

TIP | CAN I MIX STERLING SILVER WITH MY FINE SILVER CLAY?

Some brands of fine silver metal clay offer firing directions that mention top temps of 1490° F (810° C). These instructions were originally designed to include sterling silver wire additions to metal clay, hence the temperature just below 1500° F (816° C). You may choose to use sterling silver for your embeds if you feel that the tensile strength of the wire is more important than being able to forge or manipulate your fine silver base. All fine silver metal clays will offer the maximum density and tensile strength when they are fully fired and treated to the two-hour deep annealing soak at 1650° F (899° C). If you choose to include sterling silver in your fine silver clay firings, you may need to drop your firing temperatures as low as 1200°F (649° C) if you're using fine gauge sterling silver wire, if you're using fine gauge sterling silver wire, or if your sterling is of lower quality and might contain nickel or zinc.

Top, a greenware maison in the French style, complete with tiny shutters and gable ornament. Bottom, First Kiss pipe rings, one fired and finished, and a greenware ring ready for the kiln.

and cast it, as an ingot or into a mold; or toss it in water and let it make slip (see *Slip*, page 132). Alternatively, you can laboriously rehydrate it by chopping it finely, adding water, kneading it in, and letting it rest. You may have to repeat this process several times over the course of a week to achieve a workable clay body.

Water works well to rehydrate dried clay, but isn't particularly effective on wet clay. When I teach metal clay classes, I can always spot the students who are wheel-throwers or who have been taught to use water on their fresh clay, because their hands are covered in slip and their pieces are frequently stuck to their drying boards. I personally never get fresh clay wet unless I'm doing an appliqué that requires the flexibility of a very fresh clay piece to bond to something with texture.

The best way to avoid being tempted to overwater is to handle the clay correctly in the first place. Keep in mind that just your touch will speed the drying process. Also, whatever is on your skin and your work surface will be worked into

becomes unworkable. For instance, if you decide to give up on what you're making, you can re-roll the partially dry clay with some fresh, moist clay, and let it sit in a tightly capped plastic cup (see *Storage Containers*, page 17) overnight. For best results, don't add more than 10% dry clay to 90% fresh, or you may find that instead of rejuvenating your old clay, you have ruined your fresh.

If your clay has dried completely, you have options, too: fire the lump and turn it in for scrap; melt it with your torch

TIP | MINDFULNESS

To keep your clay in good condition, it's best to work on just one component at a time, devoting your full attention to it with no interruptions. The more attention you can give to your fresh clay, the less attention it will need when it becomes dry clay or fired metal. Proceeding more mindfully when your clay is fresh will actually save you time in the middle and end stages of the work, and will give you a healthier work environment by allowing you to skip the filing and sanding, if desired.

your clay, so I tend to avoid products like bag balms and heavy ointments. To keep my clay moist and pure, I make sure my hands are clean, dry, and lubricated with a very small amount of olive oil. Just use a bit of oil—if your hands feel slippery, you're wearing too much. If your hands stick to the clay, or dry it out on contact, you need a little more oil. If you're working in a hot, dry location, you might want to add a humidifier to your room. If you're working on a sunny table, move your work out of the direct sunlight. You have to actively collaborate with your clay to keep it fresh and willing, and, if you want to work with the clay like I do, you may have to unlearn some of what you have been taught to do.

It can be difficult to break bad habits in clay handling, especially if your first classes completely skipped the concept, but I promise you it's worth your time to learn to leave out the water and dramatically cut your handling of the clay. Not only will you save time and money by not wasting or having to re-hydrate clay, but you will do yourself a favor by cutting down on the amount of metal you absorb through your skin. When you're covered in wet metal clay or slip, you absorb the silver through your pores. Drinking colloidal silver is harmless, as it passes through your digestive tract, but absorbing silver into your skin is a different matter; it's not beneficial, and is, in fact, the quickest path to silver poisoning. The 2008 news stories on the man who turned blue from bathing his skin in colloidal silver are recommended reading on this topic. Having one's hands covered in wet metal slip is not a serious matter if it's occasional, but it should be an informed choice, not a default, because it could have serious health implications if the body in question has a delicate immune system, is expecting a baby, or is already possessed of a toxic load of metal. So, you might like to skip the mess and learn to work dry.

tools

I keep my workbench simple when I'm working with metal clay. I don't use additives or have any special unguents to keep the clay pliable longer. I don't buy any slips, slurries, extruders, oil-based repair goos, or extenders. I just use the metal clay right out of the packet and keep my clay from sticking to my tools and work surface with a very thin coat of olive oil. There are several tools that any metal clay craftsperson shouldn't do without.

WORKING SURFACE. I've seen quite a variety of working surfaces for metal clay. Some people use marked cutting mats, some choose glass or Plexiglass sheets, others prefer silicon or Teflon mats. I like a flexible work surface that can stand up to a blade, so I generally work on 6" (15 cm) squares of Teflon. You can buy Teflon in any cooking store; it's generally sold in sizes that will line cookie sheets or baking dishes. It's easy to cut down with ordinary scissors.

CLAY ROLLERS. To roll my clay, I use a tube of ½" (1.3 cm) PVC pipe cut into a 6" (15.2 cm) section. Some people enjoy using the metal tubes meant for making crepes, found in fine kitchen stores, still others prefer clear plastic or wood rollers.

A simple and inexpensive clay roller is ½" (1.3 cm) PVC pipe, with the cut edges sanded smooth.

I like the PVC because it's cheap, slender, and doesn't stick to the clay.

ROLLING GUIDES. Traditionally, metal clay artists have used stacked playing cards, set side by side about 2" (5.2 cm) apart, to form a width guide for rolling their clay. The clay is set in the center of the stacks, and when rolled, the resulting shape has a uniform thickness. So many people have been encouraged to use playing cards as rolling guides that many of my students still ask, "How many cards thick is that?" which is why I mention my rolling thicknesses throughout this book in the number of cards that my roll corresponds to.

To be honest, playing cards are dreadful rolling guides; they warp, compress, and get damp, and are too short to support a roll of clay long enough to make strap bands or ring shanks. So if you're serious about your metal clay work, don't use cards; choose firm guides instead.

You can make your own rolling guides out of metal slats, cut down to 6" (15.2 cm) lengths, or get yourself one of these nifty sets of color-coded rolling guides. I use these guides exclusively when I work, and it's handy because each one corresponds to a certain number of "cards." If you're an instructor, these color-coded guides are invaluable for helping your students easily understand how thickly you want them to roll and texture their sheets of clay.

RUBBER STAMPS + TEXTURE PLATES. I use rubber stamps, brass texture plates, and a whole lot of black rubber texture sheets to texture my clay. The stamps and rubber texture sheets must be oiled or sprayed with a nonstick coating before use. I like to use a light rub of olive oil for this

because it evaporates cleanly from the stamps, never leaving them sticky. If you're using olive oil spray, which I love, never spray your stamps directly. Simply spray a bit on your palms, rub your hands together, and then rub the surface of your stamps.

CUTTERS. I use cutter sets and thin-walled pastry cutters with no seams for small shapes, chain links, and clasps, and flexible 4¾" (12.1 cm) medical tissue blades to cut flat sheet, bevels, flat band ring shanks, box sides, and chain links. For cutting small holes or the centers out of small rings, I use a variety of cocktail straws and teeny brass cutters. I'll admit, I collect drinking and cocktail straws everywhere I go and become excited when I see a new one. Clean, sharp cutters will make all of the difference in making clean, sharp cuts.

Texture sheets and a large rubber stamp block.

A variety of cutters; *clockwise* a four-petal flower from a cake decorating set, a one-inch round from a doughnut cutter set, three round Kemper Klay Kutters, and a professional Matfer pastry cutter.

Amazingly, at the time I write this, there are still no mass-produced professional metal clay cutters on the market. Especially lacking in our world are "donut" cutters; cutters that have a center punch to cut out a link or ring in one motion. It's very difficult to achieve precise center cuts by eyeballing them, so as more professional jewelers play with metal clay, I imagine that the market will catch up with the demand for better cutter sets, especially if you join me in asking for them! Because most instructors don't emphasize the need for making clean cuts, many people don't know what a difference they can make.

MOLDS. I make texture sheets and molds with silicone molding compound. It's neat stuff that comes in two parts, like an epoxy. You use an equal amount of each to knead small balls together until they are an even color. You can then form patties for button-style molds, or roll the compound out like clay to make impressions. When properly mixed, the molding compound is virtually indestructible after curing and won't stick to your tools or the metal clay.

SMALL PAINT BRUSH. It's true in every circumstance that the nicer your brush is, the finer your work can be. I like to use synthetic sable brushes, about ¼" (6 mm) wide, with bristles that are ¼" to ⅜" (6 to 9 mm) long. Invest in a nice brush or two. If you buy synthetics, you can get two for under $10. Nice brushes won't drop bristles in your work and don't leave brushstrokes behind.

OLIVE OIL. Olive oil is a great lubricant to use so your clay won't stick to your fingers and tools. It won't leave your tools or stamps sticky, like some sprays and balms will, but it *can* dissolve the clay and make a real mess, just like water. Don't use an excessive amount on your hands or tools. Spray your hands lightly with oil, rub them together, and then rub your *lightly* oiled hands on your work surface, roller, and nonsilicone texturing tools before beginning to work. Repeat as often as necessary throughout the work process. I generally oil a thing and then wipe it with a towel. This leaves a thin nonstick surface that won't add oil to your

Texture sheets made from two-part silicone molding compound.

working clay. If you end up working too much oil into the clay, you'll change its chemical composition and may find the clay no longer workable.

STORAGE CONTAINERS. They're meant for holding leftover oil or acrylic paint, cost only pennies each, and seal completely to keep in the moisture. They come in two sizes to hold exactly ½ or 1 ounce (14 or 28 g) of metal clay each. Using these cups I can keep opened metal clay fresh for months. I have no idea how I ever managed without them.

BEADING AWL. A slender, sharp probe, useful for reaming and cleaning holes or making pilot holes for later drilling.

PLIERS. I use four sets of pliers every day in my studio: a heavy-duty round-nose, a regular round-nose with long, ergonomic handles, and two flat-nosed pliers, also with long handles.

WRAP + TAP TOOL. This ingenious hand tool provides not only a hardened steel barrel for forming or coiling wire, but a plastic-coated gripping jaw that won't mar your metal. Get the set of two, with three barrels each, for a total of six hard steel cylinder sizes in two easy-to-use pliers-style tools.

WIRE STRAIGHTENERS. The nylon jaws of this type of pliers are removable so they can be replaced when they get chewed up. I use these pliers not only for straightening wire, but for holding pieces that I don't want to mar.

FLUSH CUTTERS. I think I've bought every type of cutter on the market, but now just have one in my toolkit. It's crucial that your cutters be strong, sharp, and make perfect flush cuts if you want to fuse or solder your pieces.

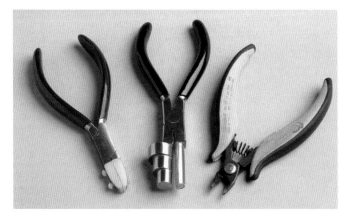

Left to right: A nylon-jaw plier, meant for holding metal without marking it or for straightening wire; a Wrap and Tap tool, meant for forming curves or coils; and my favorite flush cutter. I now use this single cutter for everything I do at the bench.

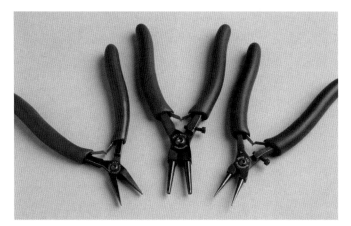

Three workhorse pliers from Swanstrom: a flat-nose *(left),* a heavy-duty round-nose *(middle),* and a regular round-nose *(right).* These are my favorite pliers on the market.

BRASS OR STEEL BRUSH. I only use soft brass brushes on my fine silver work, although I know that many people have been taught to use stiffer steel brushes. I like the softer brass brushes because they don't rust, which allows me to brush my metal wet without being concerned about ruining my brushes, and because they don't stab me cruelly every time I pick them up. Brushes rapidly wear down and need to be replaced. I buy them by the dozen.

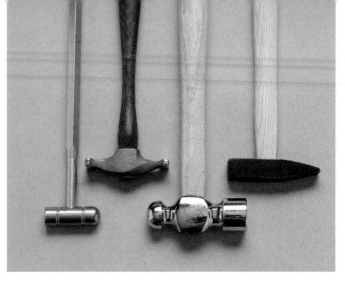

BURNISHER. Burnishers come in all shapes and sizes: some are long and resemble a beading awl, some are shaped like rounded scoops, and some are small hand-held stones or pieces of metal harder than that being burnished. Pieces of agate are sometimes used to burnish greenware, with interesting effect.

SANDING PAPERS + CLOTHS. I don't do much sanding, but when I do, I generally prefer to use a small piece of very fine sandpaper or a salon board meant for synthetic nails. Each of these has a very fine grit.

TUMBLER. A tumbler is an essential tool for a metal studio; it can be loaded with many types of tumbling media and can easily clean an oxide surface or produce anything from a gleam to a mirror-finish shine on your silver. While I love large vibratory tumblers with easy reach-in lids, most home studios don't have room in their shops or their budgets for one. I don't. Instead, I use an amazingly inexpensive and sturdy rock tumbler. I fill my tumbler with 1 lb (0.5 kg) of mixed stainless steel shot, some water, and a little Dawn dishwashing liquid. I generally use it in 15-minute increments to clean and polish, or as long as overnight for ear wires, headpins, or rivets. A tumbler won't really work-harden your pieces, but it can produce a very clean and burnished surface on your metal.

Four hammers *(left to right):* a small, lightweight brass hammer, useful for work-hardening bails and tiny chain links, a high-end texturing hammer, an inexpensive chasing hammer, and a nice 8 oz riveting hammer, perfect for fine silver. I could get by with only my riveting hammer, or a nice goldsmithing hammer, if I had to choose only one.

Tumbler

HAMMERS. I use four different hammers in my everyday work: a small, lightweight brass hammer, for getting into tight places and for use on delicate pieces; a German chasing hammer, with a wide, flat round head; a heavy chasing hammer; and a chisel-point riveting hammer. Each of these has its place in my work and is chosen not only for head shape but for weight. The world is full of hammers; buy good ones, and find ones that fit your hand. Most serious metalsmiths finish their own hammer faces by grinding and polishing to taste, but I admit that mine are straight out of the box.

ANVIL. I have a variety of anvils in sizes ranging from a little stainless steel 3" (7.6 cm) cutie to a massive 28 lb (13 kg) forming anvil with a long, curved horn. My workhorse anvil, however, is a 6 lb (2.7 kg), smoothly finished stainless steel anvil with a graduated horn. I'm also partial to my rough steel anvil, purchased for just a few dollars at a discount tool house. Each anvil or hammering surface has its own appeal, and I choose which one I want to use based on its weight, finish, and horns or holes. It would be difficult to get by with only one anvil.

RING MANDREL. Don't be tempted to skimp on this graduated tool used for sizing rings. Buy a good, solid one, preferably with size markings carved into the barrel. If you set stones into your work, you'll want to have both a plain mandrel and one with a groove cut down the center to protect gemstone points while working the band of a ring. Ring mandrels come in shapes as well; you may enjoy using oval or square mandrels to shape your metal clay or wire ring shanks.

BEZEL MANDREL. I use a slender round bezel mandrel in spaces that my ring mandrel is too large to fit, like inside chain links that I'm work-hardening or texturing, to wrap graduated coils, and to form cones. Again, don't skimp on this tool; it's a lifetime piece, so buy a good one.

METAL HOLE PUNCH. I use a simple two-hole punch for my work—the two hole sizes are suitable for the majority of my punching needs. Punches come in all styles and sizes.

DRILL. I use a simple hand drill for most of my work, although sometimes, if I have a lot to do, I use a Dremel or a flexible shaft tool to speed the process. When I work with metal clay, I usually make my holes in fresh or bone-dry clay, and have no need of a drill, although I sometimes use drill bits, and twist them by hand, to make tiny holes in leather-hard or bone-dry clay.

Blazer professional torch and a kiln brick, for fusing fine silver wire.

A slender bezel mandrel, useful for forming bezels, graduated coils, or for supporting small chain links in the work hardening process.

TORCH. I am devoted to my professional-quality, hand-held, portable, refillable butane torches. I do have a professional mixed-fuel Little Torch set up at my bench, although I admit that I rarely light it anymore; my butane torches can handle most jobs. I turn to my professional torch when I need a tiny, pinpoint flame, hotter than 1800° F (982° C).

KILN BRICK. A kiln brick is an invaluable tool in a fine silver studio. It can be used for almost any fusing job or to draw large or petal-shaped beads on the end of wire. Kiln bricks can be purchased from most clay or kiln supply houses, are about the size and shape of a regular red brick, and can easily be cut with a wire or fine saw to your desired working size.

THIRD HAND OR TWEEZERS. Third Hands, locking tweezers, and protective fiber tweezers are all used to support or immobilize work in the flame. A kiln brick can, in most circumstances described in this book, take the place of the Third Hand and locking tweezers, because most fine silver work can be laid directly on the brick, with extraneous parts tucked away into channels dug in the soft brick.

basic techniques

The basic techniques used when working with metal clay are what are known in the clay world as hand-building skills. Hand-building is very different from wheel-throwing because it rarely involves the use of water or slip for anything other than manual joinery on leather-hard or bone-dry clay, while wheel-throwers use water with clay in all stages, and lots of it. Hand-building skills are used with every type of clay body, and many of the tools that we use to cut or manipulate the clay are the same as those you would find in a traditional clay studio. Making smooth balls, rolling and texturing even sheets of clay, and rolling snakes and coils are all methods you will use to do the projects in this book.

Beautifully smooth rolled balls of fresh fine silver metal clay.

ROLLED BALLS + SIMPLE SHAPES. Perhaps the motion I use most as a metal clay artist is a swift, clean, compressive roll of a piece of clay into a smooth ball with no cracks. I use this technique to keep my clay fresh in its little container, but also to make and start many design elements or components. I also like to begin with a smooth, compressed ball of clay before I roll a sheet of clay for texturing, as this helps eliminate problems associated with rerolling poorly joined leftover scraps of clay and the air bubbles that can result from careless handling.

Unless your design aesthetic involves cracked surfaces (which can be lovely) or you intend to sand and file each of your pieces (which, because I love you and want you to stay healthy, I don't recommend), you need to start each metal clay project smoothly to finish smoothly, so perfecting the cleanly rolled ball is key. Give yourself time to master this technique and don't give up; learning it is the best thing you can give yourself as a metal clay artisan.

The challenge is to achieve your desired form with as little handling as possible. Nothing dries the clay like your touch, so if you want it to remain malleable and smooth, it's up to you to touch it as little as possible. Your goal is to be able to pick up your clay scraps, firmly compress them between your palms, and then quickly roll them up into a ball or egg shape, all in about three seconds or less. The real secret is pressure, and lots of it, not a lot of rolling. I find that some people like to meditate on their next move by holding or rolling their working clay in their hands; these people also frequently have a problem with overdry clay.

TIP | ROLLED BALL USES

Smoothly rolled balls of clay made into **HEAD PINS**; embedded in a **STACKED RING**; let to dry as little egg shapes and embedded in slurry and bone-dry clay pieces for a **NEST PENDANT** and a **PARK RING**, complete with boulders.

| head pins | stacked ring | nest pendant | park ring |

This technique is important for a couple of reasons. First, when you roll sheets of clay, beginning with a smooth ball will produce a smoothly rolled sheet, free of air bubbles or cracks. Second, a smooth ball with no cracks, tucked away in an air-tight storage container, has only one surface. Metal clay stored in this way—as opposed to just stuffed into the packet it came in as wads or scraps—will retain as much moisture as possible and, amazingly, can stay fresh for months.

TIP | PRACTICE CLAY

If you'd like to practice rolling smooth clay balls or any other ma-neuver with fine silver metal clay, I suggest buying a small quantity of porcelain clay. The two clay bodies have much the same feel, and dry and crack in about the same amount of time.

Roll balls and eggs in various sizes, from the size of seed beads to the size of peas. Stack them up like tiny cannonballs and let them dry as is; these rolled balls won't go to waste. You can stick pieces of 18-, 16- or 14-gauge fine silver wire into the smoothest ones while they're fresh and fire them fully to make ball-end head pins (see *Head Pins*, page 44). If you have a nice supply of both dried balls and fired ball-end head pins, you'll have lots of lovely choices to work with when it's time to build a little forest of silver fruit trees, a miniature rocky beach, a nest full of eggs, or a faux rivet (see *Ball-End Faux Rivets*, page 78). When you can roll a smooth ball of clay quickly and without effort, you are ready to handle the clay professionally.

ROLLED SHEETS. It's important to practice rolling smooth, even sheets since you'll use this technique in almost everything you make from metal clay. To roll out, set two rolling guides (page 15) onto your work surface, one size (or two cards) thicker

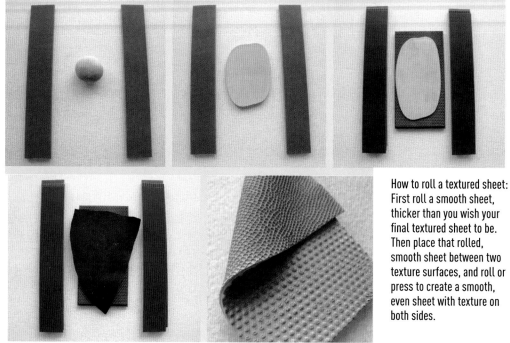

How to roll a textured sheet: First roll a smooth sheet, thicker than you wish your final textured sheet to be. Then place that rolled, smooth sheet between two texture surfaces, and roll or press to create a smooth, even sheet with texture on both sides.

than your desired sheet thickness. Place the guides on each side of the clay lump. Use a roller (page 17) to smooth the lump into a sheet. Switch to the next smallest rolling guide size to roll your final thickness, or press or roll the sheet with a stamp or texture sheet (page 15). **NOTE** *If you'd like texture on both sides of your sheet, place the sheet between two textures, and press or roll them both at once. It's important that your clay sheet remain even in thickness, so beware of thick and thin spots if you're working between two textured surfaces.*

SNAKES. Snakes of clay are used either as a surface ornament (see the ring shank on page 53), to strengthen the joints in a box form, or to fill a gap. Joint fills like this are used routinely in regular clay work, but rarely in metal clay because metal clay pieces are, in general, so small that the joins don't require support. However, if yours do, or if you have a gap to fill, a tiny rolled snake, pressed into the wetted bone-dry or hard leather-hard join or gap, and then

smoothed with a tiny bit of slip or water, will do the job. You may enjoy using silicone-tipped watercolor blenders for this job (see *Resources*, page 138).

To roll a snake, place a smooth ball of clay on the working surface and lightly press it with your fingertips. Quickly move your hand forward and backward until the ball forms a cylinder of desired size and length. Never stretch or pull the metal clay. You don't want to build weak sections into your work, and pulling the clay does exactly that: it makes thin spots in the finished metal. If you want a longer or a

It's easy to roll snakes of metal clay with your fingertips to make toggle bars or tiny little snakes to reinforce box joins.

A simple circle, cut out of a rolled sheet of metal clay.

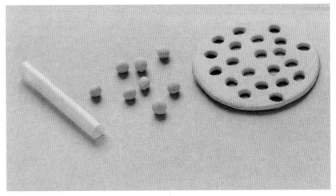

To roll balls of the same size, use a cocktail straw or tiny cutter to cut the same amount out of an evenly rolled sheet of clay.

thinner snake, roll it, don't pull it. As you compress and roll the clay, the snake will lengthen.

CUTTING. Cutting clean shapes out of rolled metal clay slabs is another important skill that many students aren't taught. When you use good cutting tools (page 15) and "heal" the cuts by gently stroking the edges, you'll have clean finished cuts without having to sand or file to get them.

It's best to texture your clay before you cut it, as you can distort your cut shapes if you texture them after cutting. In general, it's good practice to fully plan your pieces before you create them so you can make the most sensible decisions about rolling, texturing, and cutting.

Making holes in your pieces can be done at any stage. If you want extremely precise, tiny holes in your finished pieces, drilling them bone-dry or after firing with a hand drill works well, but you lose the metal from the hole as it becomes dust on your bench. If you can work with slightly

larger holes, they can be easily made in fresh clay with a tiny cocktail straw, then cleaned or reamed to size with a bead awl for a very precise look. Cutting holes in fresh clay offers the advantage of easily removing the bit of clay from the straw for later use. When I cut holes with a cocktail straw, I usually take that opportunity to roll the leftover clay into little balls and let them dry for later use as faux rivets (*Ball-End Faux Rivets*, page 78) or eggs for a nest.

SQUIDGING. If this isn't a real word, it should be. Squidging is firmly entrenched in the vocabulary of most clay artists because it perfectly describes the motion of using pressure while rubbing and worming a piece of clay onto another piece of clay, using the advantage of water or slip to make the surfaces sticky. Squidging is an active process, and the amount of pressure you use to move the pieces against each other will depend entirely on how dry and/or how fragile they are.

In traditional clay work, you'd score the pieces to be joined, apply water or slip, and then squidge the two pieces together. Scoring involves scraping or roughing up a clay surface to make it grabbier, but metal clay will not thank you for this. Skip the scoring and, in most cases, skip the slip. With metal clay, you can squidge leather-hard to bone-dry pieces together using just a small amount of water to bond their

Assemble your buildings or box pieces one slab at a time, and wait for each side to set up before you add the next.

cleanly cut edges. Wet both areas of the pieces to be joined, wait just a moment for the clay to absorb the water and get sticky, then rub the pieces together, using as much pressure as is sensible. When you first move the pieces against each other they'll slip and slide, but they will rapidly get sticky and begin to grab. When they stop moving, they're bonded. At this point, take a damp, clean paintbrush and smooth the joint on each side. If you used slip, you'll probably have a bit of a mess to mop up. If you used a moderate amount of water, just a swipe on each side should do it.

You'll know if you haven't used enough water to squidge your join together if the pieces don't really slip and slide, or if you can't feel the active moment of grabbing. Practice joining pieces together at different stages of dryness, with different amounts of water, to understand the right balance of wet and dry for this job.

APPLIQUÉ. Appliqué is the technique used to ornament greenware (unfired metal clay) with other pieces of greenware. Using a little slip or water as a bonding agent, the clay bonds quite readily with other unfired pieces of clay at any stage of dryness. Water is sufficient for most appliqué; just wet both pieces and slip, slide, and squidge them together until you feel them grab. Don't just lay the pieces together and expect them to bond, as if you were gluing. Making a permanent attachment, one that can't be knocked apart or easily broken, is an active process.

You'll find that some appliqués like to go onto bone-dry clay (page 131), some onto leather-hard (page 15). It's rare that you'd choose to appliqué when either piece is fresh and soft, but sometimes, when filling gaps or adhering to an uneven surface, the flexibility of fresh clay is just what you need to make a clean connection. Appliquéing dry balls to a fresh clay piece is a great technique to master. First, gently form

TIP | FLOATING BALLS

If you want the fine silver balls to appear to sit or float on top of the surface of a piece, don't use a dry-clay appliqué technique. Instead, embed short ball-end head pins, either made by drawing beads on fine silver wire with a torch (see **DRAWING A BEAD**, page 67) or by firing a metal clay ball onto the wire (see **HEAD PINS**, page 44) into your piece. Don't drop already fired balls into your wet divots. You may succeed in gluing the balls in place, but if you attempt to forge or form the piece after firing, they will probably pop right out. Finished metal balls can only be professionally applied to your metal clay piece by embedding them as ball-end head pins or after firing, using solder.

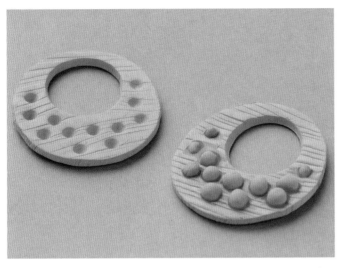

Smoothly rolled and dried balls of fine silver metal clay are placed in wetted divots, to seat them snugly in place. The finished, fired balls can be left round or hammered.

small divots in the freshly rolled clay with a ball-end burnisher. Make your divots deep enough to fully seat the bottom of the dry balls. **NOTE** *To make divots in fresh clay without damaging a texture on the back side of your piece, let the piece air dry for 15 minutes to an hour (depending on your humidity) on a sheet of Teflon, plastic, or glass, with the textured side up and the future divot side down. This will allow your divot side to remain fresh and soft, while the back surface with the texture on it air-dries. When the back surface is nice and dry, flip the piece over. The divot side, if it was snug against the Teflon, plastic, or glass sheet, should still be fresh and soft enough to place your divots, and the action of doing so will not damage the now-dry surface texture on the back.*

Add a drop of water to each divot, just enough to fill it to the rim. Use tweezers to place a completely dry ball of clay into each divot, let the ball sit in the wet divot for a moment to get sticky, then press down on it gently. Rotate the ball a bit until you feel it stick in the clay. Mop up the excess water with a bit of torn paper towel or a cotton swab. Once the piece dries, the balls should be completely bonded in their divots. If you can easily flick off the embedded balls prior to firing, they weren't embedded properly in the first place. Each ball should be so well bonded that you should have to dig and pry them out if you want to remove them. **NOTE** *If yours aren't fully bonded, either your divots weren't deep enough to properly seat the balls, you didn't use enough water, or perhaps you didn't remember to press and roll them a bit in their wetted divots.*

firing

As I mentioned at the beginning of this chapter, there are several different brands and many different formulas of fine silver metal clay on the market. There's also plenty of conflicting information on firing times and temperatures to go along with those choices. It's actually very simple: no matter what kind of silver clay you're using, it's just a collection of pure fine silver particles, and, as such, it sinters, fuses, and flows at very predictable temperatures.

I recommend firing all fine silver metal clays at 1650° F (899° C) for two full hours. With this combination of temperature and time, the maximum finished density can be attained. In the first stages of firing, the binder material burns out completely, and the metal particles sinter together. In a short *sintering* session, such as 10 or 20 minutes in the kiln, the particles adhere but aren't really fully bonded together. The extra time in the heat of a full firing acts as a deep annealing soak (see

3 DIFFERENT RINGS, 3 DIFFERENT APPLIQUÉS

Appliqué is a particularly nice technique to ornament ring shanks, to cover or border holes, or to attach simple dry clay bezel wells for resin pours or stone setting. The three rings shown here include ball, ring, bar, and bezel appliqués.

BALLS (above)

The little gathering of silver balls shown in this **NEST RING** was made by letting the appliquéd piece set up, filling the dry well of the center ring with thick slip, and dropping in dry egg-shaped balls of clay. After the nest and eggs dried completely, I recoated the eggs with plenty of slip and let them dry again, then repeated the coating twice more. These layers of slip give the eggs a deep glow after firing, in addition to making sure they are adequately stuck together.

BARS + BEZELS (right)

Whenever possible, appliqué a ring band while it's still flat, as I did with the railroad-track band on the right. You'll have the best luck embellishing with tiny bars like this when you wait until the clay pieces are leather-hard to bone-dry; placing ornaments like this when the clay is fresh and wet is rather frustrating. After you fire the band, bend it around a ring mandrel to show off the beautiful textural definition of the bars. Note how the shank employs four bars placed in a square to form a bezel; this can be used to set a photo with resin—a very easy way to include unexpected excitement in your piece.

RINGS (top)

The **KANDINSKY RING** was made to match the **AMPHORA PENDANT** (page 121). It features a simple rectangular pad appliquéd with small, thick ringlets, and sports a previously fired, formed, and embedded ring shank (page 52.) A dry ball of clay was squidged into place inside each appliquéd ring with a few drops of water. The middle photo shows the freshly fired white oxide surface, and the right photo features the patinated and tumbled finished piece.

Annealing, page 133) and is crucial to the stability and strength of your finished pieces. This two-hour heat soak strengthens your pieces because it allows the metal particles to fully bond (although still without actually melting together) as the boundaries of the metal grains merge. With a full firing, minor flaws and gaps in the metal matrix heal themselves, the number of metal grains diminishes, and your finished piece will be able to stand up to forming and forging. An underfired or short-fired piece is likely to break if you attempt to change its shape because it is built of many small particles of silver, joined together at the edges. A properly made, fully sintered and fully annealed metal clay piece should be able to stand up to any traditional metalsmithing technique.

INCLUSIONS. Rather than choosing to underfire or short-fire your metal clay to include nonmetal embellishments (many of which would melt or crack at such high temperatures), consider building your work in a different way. You can, for example, make or buy professional prong and bezel settings, or insert rivet posts or individual handmade prongs, and then place your stones, cabs, or beads professionally in your metal after a proper firing. If you have metal clay pieces that were previously underfired and don't contain any glass, gemstone, or nonmetal embellishments, you can refire them fully at any time. Just place them in a kiln for a two-hour soak at 1650° F (899° C), or, if you don't own a kiln, take them to a metal clay studio and specifically request a full firing. You'll need to work-harden them again, of course, and re-apply any patina or surface finish.

KILNS. I recommend firing all metal clay work in a digitally controlled electric kiln for best results. Anything that's torch-fired, short-fired, or underfired, as I mentioned previously, will be inferior in terms of strength and durability, and if your kiln accidentally overfires, it can melt your work down into small puddles of metal. Torch-firing is not something I recommend under any circumstance; not only does it produce an inferior metal product, but if you aren't outdoors or don't have professional ventilation, you end up breathing the fumes of combustion and, as you'll see from reading the metal clay packet directions, this is not recommended. Burning metal clay binder is a respiratory irritant, and you should not be in the room with the pieces in the first 20 to 30 minutes of firing.

You can save up your greenware (unfired clay work) and take it to a studio for firing, or you can buy your own kiln. It can be confusing to shop for the right kiln: you need to decide if you'll also use it for fusing or annealing glass, for firing gold, or

A Sea Prong element holding a cut peridot in organic fine silver wire prongs, which were embedded into the fresh wet clay sculpture on the end of a curled fine silver wire.

for firing high-temperature clays as well. It's possible to choose one kiln to do everything, or you can purchase different appliances to handle each facet of your studio work.

A Paragon PMC kiln, one of several brands on the market.

ELECTRIC KILNS that hold a temperature of 1650° F (899° C) for two hours, without fluctuating too many degrees in either direction, are your best choice, especially those created specifically for metal clay. These specialty kilns have small chambers, precise digital controllers, and come to temperature quickly.

One of the electric kilns I use is made by Paragon and is one of a series that are specifically designed to fire metal clay. These little kilns are expensive, over $500, and much of the price is driven by the high-quality digital controllers that are built in.

LAMPWORKING KILNS will certainly work for firing metal clay, as long as they are electric, but they generally have larger chambers and use more power to heat.

ANNEALING BOXES made for lampworkers, such as the toolbox models, usually can't get hot enough to fully fire metal clay. I have a popular toolbox annealer that has a top temperature of about 1200° F (649° C). I find this annealer only useful for metal clay for short, lower-temperature firings meant to stabilize greenware for travel to a kiln that can fully fire the work.

GAS KILNS are generally inappropriate for firing metal clay, due to their flame-driven temperature fluctuations. If your kiln temperature jumps too high, even briefly, you can lose your surface texture to slumping or partial melting.

TIP | CAN I MULTITASK MY KILN?

Glass artists often ask if using their glass kiln to fire metal clay will leave a residue that can pollute their kiln or "silver-fume" their glass. The answer is absolutely not, as long as you are firing your metalwork at a high enough temperature to burn out all metal clay binder residue. A short, or low-temperature firing may not be hot enough or long enough to completely cleanse the kiln of the soot and carbon from the burned binder. A complete firing at 1650° F (899° C) results in complete combustion, leaving only pure metal and a clean kiln.

There is no danger of silver-fuming your glass beads, unless you both overfire your metal and melt your glass into a pool. Silver doesn't vaporize at the temperatures used to anneal glass, so even if there was silver residue in your kiln, it wouldn't be able to mobilize onto your glass unless you brought it to a temperature over 1760° F (960° C).

If you plan, however, on underfiring or short-firing your metal clay, and want to avoid scumming your glass with trace residue from uncombusted soot and carbon, you'll need a separate kiln for each medium, or you'll simply need to take your kiln up to full temperature (1650° F [899° C]) between metal clay firings and glass annealing cycles in order to burn the kiln clean.

finishing

How you finish your work is what will really mark it as your own. You have many choices: will your work be matte, shiny, or a combination of both? Will your edges be sharp and clean, or gently rounded? Will your metal be patinated, blackened, shiny silver, or sport a finish that shows some of the white oxide from the firing process?

Most people want to finish their pieces with a clean surface; they want their metal to be smooth and to appear well-made, with no rough edges. The easiest way to achieve this is to keep your work tight as your pieces progress. I puzzle over why so many metal clay students are taught to make sloppy cuts and rough joins, then sand, file, and fill them later. Sanding dry clay, as I mentioned before, is not only unhealthy, but also time-consuming and a waste of material. It's really much easier (and more efficient in terms of time and money) to work cleanly. I tend to think of my "finish" as something that begins with my start; even when I am cutting the raw clay, I'm thinking about the final edges. If you've been taught not to care about how you begin a project, and to think only of the end, you might experiment with being mindful and curious at every stage of your work because I think you might get a better sense of the possibilities of your pieces if the beauty of your work is showing through at every step. Making clean cuts and wasting as little material as possible are marks of good craftsmanship, no matter what material is being worked. For example, can you imagine woodworking students being taught to make sloppy cuts in wood, and then spend the time to sand and plane the pieces down after cutting and to fill gaps in their joinery with wood fiber filler?

Choices that you make in construction can affect the finished surface of your pieces. How you handle the clay may affect how your pieces polish up or how they take patina. The way you touch the clay, whether or not you use slip, whether or not you had perfume, oil, or lotion on your hands when you were working the fresh clay, whether you rubbed or burnished the surface before firing—all of these can affect your final finish. If you've ever seen odd spots in your patinated surface, or if you've had areas of your metal that simply won't take a stain in the same way as their surrounding areas, you are probably seeing the chemical result of lotions or oils that were on your skin. If you use cheap butane in your torch when fusing, the fuel can spit and stain the metal, or if you burnish a piece before or after firing, it won't absorb patina as deeply, or maybe not at all. Pay attention to cause and effect; things that cause problems, can, if understood, be controlled and used to your advantage or avoided.

A golden patina on a **CIRCLET OF FLOWERS** piece. See the project on page 105.

PATINA. If you like to patinate (darken or color the surface) your work, you have several choices. Commercial silver blackening agents are nice because they work instantly, but most of them are highly toxic. If your solution has a skull and crossbones on the packaging, you might consider switching to the relatively harmless liver of sulfur. I use it on all of my work because I love the variety of colors I can get, and I'm happy to have a product that I can use safely. If you have a scientific bent, you can mix your own solution exactly to taste, beginning with distilled water, and adding in only the hard minerals that give you the color range you enjoy. Or, if you enjoy serendipity, as I do, you can mix your solution with ordinary tap water. The composition of the water from your faucet can be different on different days; if you are particularly partial to a certain batch of patina, you might consider having the water tested to see what the chemical and mineral composition is.

I usually begin the finish on my components and pieces when they're fresh out of the kiln. The white oxide surface of pieces right out of the kiln is extremely porous, so I find it a good time to add a really deep surface patina. Applying patina to the rough white oxide surface gives you the chance to achieve colors that don't appear on cleaned or polished silver, such as robin's egg blue and deep, rich, matte gold. I sometimes lightly brush my freshly fired metal clay components with a wet brass brush, or tumble them for 10 minutes with a bit of Dawn dish soap and about a pound of mixed stainless steel shot, just to clean them a bit, or I patinate them without any cleaning at all. It just depends on the look I'm going for and how much I want the patina on the exposed surface to vary from that in the crevices.

A hand-sculpted fine silver bird peers through a stylized birdhouse door.

I generally mix my liver of sulfur solution with room temperature, not hot, water, so things don't move too quickly, but I do keep a bowl of hot water handy for heating the piece (instead of the solution) and a bowl of ice water, with a bit of baking soda in it, to slow or stop the development of color. **NOTE** *Don't get baking soda in your tumbler! Rinse the pieces fully before you put them in. The baking soda causes gas expansion in the barrel of the tumbler and, if you don't catch it in time, can blow the lid right off. Messy.*

Patina can be built in layers, and I go between the patina, the tumbler, the brass brush, and the bench many times. I may burnish at any point in the process, and I may subject a piece that has already been polished and patinated to the heat of fusing, or even a refiring in an assembly. Although the heat of a torch or of the kiln does burn off patina, fine silver seems, at times, to have a chemical memory and may "remember" a previous patina, even after the heat of a full firing. This can make for interesting layers, but also for unexpected results. For example, if you choose to completely blacken your work in progress with liver of sulfur, it might not be able to take a lighter golden or bronzed patina later, even after it is refired in the kiln. Beware of going too much further than your intended finished surface, especially if you enjoy the color ranges of golds, bronzes, oranges, and coppers that liver of sulfur brings.

All finishing options are open to you in any order; there is no right or wrong way to use patina or to clean and polish your metal. The only essential step you need to take after firing is work-hardening (page 137); everything else you do to finish is optional.

safety

Fine silver metal clay is absolutely safe if used appropriately, but you should be aware of two basic common-sense safety rules when working with it. First, avoid inhalation of dust, filings, and the fumes of combustion, and second, don't cover yourself in slip or dry clay dust, as the skin is highly absorptive and silver poisoning can occur with excessive or repeated exposure.

We make judgment calls about our activities on a regular basis, especially when it comes to product safety. For example, I'm more than willing to breathe a little bit of spray sunscreen if having a spray formula means that I actually wear sunscreen to avoid skin cancer. Sometimes a little bit of toxic exposure pays off big like that. With metal clay, though, all unsafe behavior can be easily avoided, with no compromises in the finished product, no additional money spent, and no time lost. The material itself is not a danger; in fact, working with fine silver metal clay, wire, and sheet is an excellent path to a completely clean and safe metal studio.

There are only a few simple guidelines beyond the obvious (don't breathe, eat, or rub metal or metal dust into your skin) to follow for completely safe handling and firing of fine silver metal clay (and to run a responsible studio for students to enjoy). The first is to only do burnout firings—this includes all metal clay firings, not just those with burnout cores—in a well-ventilated room. If you plan to be around when you're firing, fire the kiln outdoors or leave the room. If you'll be out of the room when your clay is firing and you're only firing fine silver metal clay, it's perfectly fine to fire the kiln in your studio. The amount of smoke and fumes produced from the burning binder is small, and as long as you aren't in the room while it's burning out, it's fine. The smoke will not measurably pollute your indoor environment once it dissipates. My kilns live outdoors, but I'm fortunate to live in a warm climate.

If you're forced to fire your kiln in a classroom situation, take a break and plan on leaving the room for the first 20 to 30 minutes of your firing while the binder is burning out. Alternatively, you can load your kiln when it's hot, as one major metal clay distributor most probably did when the company ran toxicity tests of burnout cores and metal clay fumes. If you load the kiln at full firing temperature, you'll find that your emissions are completely clean. Loading a hot kiln presents its own set of dangers, though, so I'm not sure that I can recommend it. A normal ramp-up of a heating kiln (which is what most of us experience, and how

I wish those test results had been produced) will produce appreciable smoke and fumes during the time it takes the binder or core materials to completely burn out.

Second, don't torch-fire or solder without professional ventilation, and nope, your stove hood doesn't count as ventilation unless it's a professional model, vented to the outdoors. So that means don't do it on your gas range, either. If you choose to torch-fire your metal clay and you don't have real ventilation, take it outdoors or on a screened porch, well away from people who are breathing. You might consider wearing a respirator as well.

Third, never use plastic burnout materials such as Styrene, Styrofoam, or floral foam, because they emit extremely toxic fumes when burned. Styrene and polystyrene, for example, are documented to emit neurotoxins and, in some cases, human embryotoxins, when heated or burned. This is not good for you or for our increasingly fragile environment, and it's especially bad for babes in the womb. Embryotoxins, as you might guess from the name, can harm a developing fetus, so it's vital that any woman who could be pregnant (or any person who is immuno-suppressed) avoid exposure to all burning or heated plastics. Materials Data Safety (MDS) sheets are available online from the government for almost any material or chemical compound you can name.

Fourth, when firing hollow, fragile, or curved pieces in the kiln, use asbestos-free vermiculite instead of talc-fine alumina hydrate powder (which you also don't want to breathe) for support. Alumina hydrate was mysteriously promoted as a support medium for firing metal clay pieces, but it's not a safe choice. Vermiculite is inexpensive—a dollar's worth is probably a lifetime supply—and easy to find

A Dali's Summerhome ring, with a previously fired, bent, embedded ring shank, ready to fire upside down in a little clay flowerpot filled with vermiculite. Ring shanks made in this way can be built exactly to size.

at any nursery or serious garden store. It's not only safe, but it's easy to recover after firing, reusable, and it doesn't pollute your working environment or kiln with fine powder. If you have alumina hydrate in your studio, do yourself a favor and return it to your supplier to dispose of safely.

Fifth, when finishing fired metal, do any filing wet so you don't create dust at your bench. If you're in the habit of harvesting your fine silver or other metal dust, you can do this just as effectively from the bottom of a bowl of water as you can from brushing your bench top.

The good news is that with just a little bit of care it's easy to maintain a safe, clean working environment. If, as a student, you find yourself in a toxic or fume-filled situation in a classroom, speak up, or leave the room. If you get a headache from anything that you are exposed to or working on, leave the room and get some fresh air. It's not a good idea to be too shy to protect yourself. I'm sure that metal clay classes will, over time, catch up with what industry considers best practices and default to the safest working situations. As anyone who's ever faced an injury or a lawsuit knows, it's just better business to run a safe shop.

TIP | FOUR METAL CLAY BASICS

01 | Use the formula offered by your favorite brand that has the smallest metal particle size. This is usually the version that advertises the shortest firing time, but that doesn't mean you should skimp on time or temperature. Choose the short-fire formulas not because you want to short-fire, but because smaller particles sinter together into more solid pieces.

02 | Compress as you work, but never stretch the clay. Since metal clay is made up of many small particles of silver, your goal is to keep all of those little bits neatly herded together so they can fuse in the kiln. Stretching the clay as you work it pulls the metal particles apart and adds weak points to your work that express as metal fatigue. Instead of pulling the clay, compress or roll it to make it longer or wider. Texturing the clay with rubber stamps not only adds great texture, but it's wonderfully compressive. Think of yourself as a Particle Herder.

03 | Fully fire your pieces. No matter what formula you're using, fire your pieces for two full hours at 1650° F (899° C) in an electric kiln with a digital controller. Avoid embedding glass, gems, and other items into your clay that can't take the heat of a full firing. Embed fine silver settings instead and place your non-metal embellishments in the settings after firing and finishing.

04 | Work-harden everything after firing. Firing your pieces also anneals them, making them dead soft, so you'll need to work-harden them by hammering. Don't believe anyone who tells you that fine silver can never be hard enough for "real" work. Fine silver will never get as hard as sterling silver, but if you build your pieces with sufficient thickness and support, you can make beautiful, professional quality work that will stand the tests of wear and time.

elements

This section of the book focuses on essential techniques for making basic elements and simple components in metal clay and fine silver wire. You'll see that each idea is illustrated with photos that show finished components, but it's important to keep in mind that a technique can be a path of its own, worth practicing and repeating.

Although some of these jobs may not seem to have much to do with metal clay, such as drawing a bead in wire, forging, fusing fine silver chain, hammering, and piercing flattened balls of wire, these metalsmithing maneuvers are so frequently missing from the metal clay curriculum that many artisans are unaware that they can use them to take their pieces to a professional level. It's important to understand the product as metal and to understand the possibilities and limitations of fine silver in order to envision the many things you can (or shouldn't) do with metal clay.

If you're new to metal clay or metalsmithing, I suggest that you watch the enclosed DVD, then follow each of the elements in this book in order. Each skill builds on those that came before, and each project combines more and more pieces and parts. The advanced variations can entertain you now or later, depending on your level of expertise.

This simple **WAVE RING** (left) illustrates the power of planning ahead and thinking of the parts of your jewelry as a series of separate components.

01
circles + rings

MATERIALS
Fine silver metal clay

TOOLS
Work surface
Roller
Rolling guides

Texture sheets or rubber stamps
Circle cutters
Ball-end burnisher
Hammer
Anvil
Brass brush + patina solution
(optional)

CIRCLES + RINGS are some of the most essential components for making finished jewelry. You'll need them in all shapes, sizes, and weights for your work, so making rings is a good way to practice your clay skills because everything you make will be useful. If you're just beginning, I recommend dedicating at least one ounce of metal clay to rings alone. Once you get the hang of cutting rings cleanly and

giving them interesting textures, consider making free-form shapes; they can be very comfortable to wear. I hope you'll leave this section with a lovely dish full of finished rings for chain links, earrings, captured bails, and other assemblies.

01 | In order to form metal clay rings of an even thickness, it's very important to cut them from an evenly rolled sheet of clay (see *Rolled Sheets*, page 21, and *Cutting*, page 23). For your first set, roll and texture your clay, finishing with a sheet that is 4 to 6 cards thick. Work with enough clay to make the rolled sheet slightly larger than your desired cut-outs because you don't want to use the rolled edge in your finished work unless you're interested in cracks. For smooth, clean-cut edges, always cut at least ¼" (6 mm) from any slab edge.

02 | Use clay cutters or cookie cutters to cut one to three circles out of your sheet. If this is the first time you've done this, only cut one or two circles—trust me! Use sharp, clean cutters for your cutwork, and if you'd like to end up with a lot of rings from this step, start with large circles. I used a 30 mm pastry cutter to begin. I don't recommend ever using a ballpoint pen or an art blade and template for your clay cutting; you won't get clean edges, your cut pieces will be very difficult to finger-smooth, and they will probably require dry-sanding.

03 | Immediately after cutting the outside edges of the circles, roll the leftover sheet into a smooth ball with no cracks and neatly store it in a small plastic storage container with an airtight lid. Time is of the essence because the edges of your circles are already drying. You need to smooth them while they are still fresh if you want to avoid filing or sanding later.

The beginning of a whole handful of small circles and rings—two cut out fresh clay circles, each textured, and then cut to 1³⁄₁₆" (30 mm) in diameter.

04 | Pick up each circle and gently touch, pat, or stroke the outside edges. Remember that it's the bottom side of the cut that's rough, not the top side. This is why you need to actually pick up each circle to stroke it from the back side. If you do this immediately after each cut, you'll never have to file or sand your dry clay edges to clean up your cuts.

05 | After smoothing your outside cuts, use smaller cutters to cut out the interior of the rings. Don't cut your ring walls too thin if you want sturdy, stand-alone components.

06 | Pick up each cut ring one more time, turn it over, and gently touch the interior of the cut with the pad of your fingertip. One or two touches should be all it takes to smooth the cut you made and allow the ring to fire smoothly and strongly. Touching or lightly stroking the cut clay edges

TIP | FINGER RINGS

Beautiful finger rings can be made by simply cutting circle or other ring-like shapes out of fresh rolled and textured clay. Two of the rings shown above have different kinds of **FAUX RIVETS** (page 78); the one at top left received a ball-end head pin (page 21) embed cut very short; and the ring at the front center was embellished with a rolled, dried ball set into a wet divot (see **APPLIQUÉ**, page 24) and hammered after firing. The ring at top right shows evidence of being sized around a round mandrel; can you see how the center is somewhat raised, and the inner band is perfectly smooth and even?

To make a finger ring that will come out of the kiln ready to fit a size 7–8, use a 1³⁄₁₆" (30 mm) cutter for the outside of the ring and a 1" (25 mm) cutter for the inside. Smooth the cut ring with your fingers and shape it for your finger. Think beyond round; finger rings can be exciting and comfortable to wear in a variety of shapes.

heal them is not only good for the final smoothness of your piece, but it also helps compress the edges of your clay, which is structurally beneficial.

07 | Pick up the cut-out centers of your rings now and smooth their exterior edges. Cut the centers of these centers to make even smaller rings. Continue cutting the centers of the resulting rings until you have pieces of clay too small to use, and then roll the leftovers into your working ball of clay.

08 | Let your finished rings dry completely, then fire them fully, for 2 hours at 1650° F (899° C).

09 | Hammer or forge the fired rings with a chasing hammer and an anvil, and then brush, tumble, and patina them to taste.

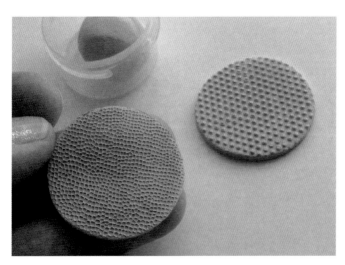

Smoothing the cut sides of the circles before cutting out their centers.

02
simple clasps + toggle bars

MATERIALS

25 g fine silver metal clay
 (of which you'll only use 10 g)
18-gauge fine silver wire

Circle or other shape cutters
Cocktail straw or tiny hole cutter
Round-nose pliers
Flush cutters
Tumbler + mixed stainless steel shot
Hammer
Anvil
Brass brush + patina solution

TOOLS

Work surface
Roller
Rolling guides
Texture sheets or rubber stamps

GREAT TOGGLE clasps are easy to make with metal clay. You only need to know a few basic steps, and those steps are ripe with possibilities: You can cut the ring hole dead center or to the side; make smaller holes for your stringing material if you like; and texture the surface to your heart's

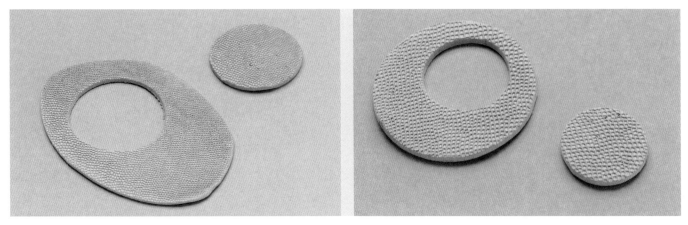

Cutting a toggle ring out of a rolled clay sheet, and then cutting the center out of the ring. This center can be rolled up to make a bar that fits the center hole perfectly. First I cut the circle out, and then I cut the center out of the first circle.

desire. The bar, if appropriately sized, can go into almost any sort of a ring for a very functional clasp and can be easily ornamented for a decorative finish.

01 | Use the rolling guides to roll the clay 6 playing cards thick. Texture the rolled sheet of clay, using rubber stamps or texture sheets, so that it ends up about 4 cards thick. You need to roll out about 25 g of clay to get a slab large enough to cut a good-sized toggle ring out, but you won't use even half of that amount in the making of a single clasp.

02 | Use a clean, sharp cookie or pastry cutter or a tissue blade to cut the outside shape of the toggle ring. I prefer cutters that cut very cleanly (like the Matfer 30 mm pastry cutter) so I don't have to do more than caress the edge to clean up the cut.

03 | Cut out the inside hole of the toggle ring—the place where the toggle bar will go. I suggest always cutting your holes in one of two sizes: $\frac{5}{8}$" (1.6 cm) or $\frac{1}{2}$" (1.3 cm). This way you can make your toggle bars all about the same length. It saves a lot of time in the long run.

04 | If desired, cut attachment holes with a cocktail straw. After each hole, ease the little bit of metal clay out of the straw and roll it into a smooth ball. You may want to let the clay balls dry and use later for faux rivets (page 78), or, if they are large enough, embed pieces of fine silver wire into them and fire them for later use as ball-end head pins (page 44) or little trees.

05 | Immediately after cutting, gently stroke the cut edges to heal them to avoid having to file or sand later.

06 | Set the toggle ring aside to dry.

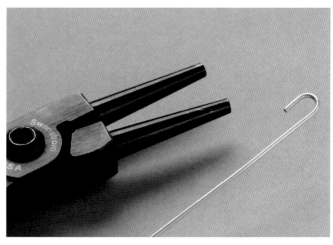

Above: a nice U turned in the end of a piece of fine silver wire. Trim this off flush to have an embeddable bail. *Below:* U bails for embedding in toggle bars, with or without added fine silver rings.

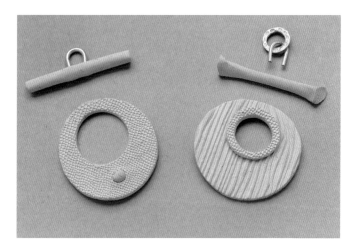

07 | Begin the toggle bar by rolling up the cut-out center circle from the ring into a smooth ball with no cracks. (I've noticed that in most cases, the amount of clay that you cut out from the center of the toggle ring is exactly the right

amount of material with which to roll a cylinder to make the toggle bar. Who knew?)

08 | Roll the ball into a cylinder that's thin enough to slip through the ring without a lot of monkeying, and long enough that it won't fall out when closed. There's no magic sizing formula for bar to ring, as every opening can be different in size or shape, so just use common sense. I personally like bars that are slender and slightly longer than the ring is wide. It's a beautiful look, very secure, and easy to use. Set the cylinder aside.

09 | Use round-nose pliers to form a bend at the end of a piece of 18-gauge wire, creating a U-shaped bail (left). Make sure the legs are long enough to fully embed into the cylinder. **NOTE** *U-bails are easiest to form if you leave the wire long and only cut it when the "U" is formed. It's easier than trying to hold on to tiny pieces of wire.*

TIP | DON'T WASTE A THING

When I made the clasps shown at left, I was careful to use each and every bit of rolled clay. I used the center cut-out from one toggle ring to make a toggle bar and used the center cut-out from the other toggle ring to form rings (see **CIRCLES + RINGS**, page 36). Then I made tiny balls with the clay I removed when cutting the attachment holes. Nothing was wasted; nothing went into the slip jar. This is how I work with metal clay, no matter what I'm making; I use every scrap of it for something and, unless I'm carving, I rarely have waste. You can never have enough pieces and parts like this if you design jewelry—they always come in handy.

10 | Embed the bail by gently pressing it into the center of the cylinder. If desired, include a small connecting ring on the U-bail before embedding it. Use any type of ring for this task as long as it's fine silver: a fused ring, a ring of fired metal clay, or a ring of bone-dry metal clay all work well.

11 | Let the ring and bar thoroughly dry. Fire fully, for 2 hours at 1650° F (899° C).

12 | If necessary after firing, clean and smooth any attachment holes with a file, burnisher, or bead awl.

13 | Work-harden the clasp and strengthen the bar's U-shaped bail and connecting ring with a hammer and anvil. Tumble, brush, and patina to taste.

Work-hardening a toggle bar bail on the side of an anvil. (Don't forget this step!)

TIP | SCULPTURAL + SHAPED TOGGLE BARS

Sculptural toggle bars, like the one with fern-frond ends (left) , take a bit of dexterity to make; the clay tends to dry very quickly and the ends of a roll don't stay flexible for too long. To make the curly ends, just roll your cylinder about ½" (1.3 cm) longer than needed on each end, and coil the ends swiftly and gently with your fingers. Embed your U-bail and set the bar aside to dry completely before firing.

This simple shaped toggle bar was made from just a plain cylinder. After shaping it, embedding the U-bail, and firing it, I hammered and forged the ends. It's a classy look, and sturdy as can be.

03
bead caps

MATERIALS

Fine silver metal clay

TOOLS

Work surface
Roller
Rolling guides
Texture sheets or rubber stamps

Circle or other shape cutters
Cocktail straw or tiny hole cutter
Wood or metal dapping block
Dapping pegs
Hammer
Brass brush, tumbler + mixed
 stainless steel shot, patina (optional)

BEAD CAPS are versatile components, and I use them for all sorts of different jewelry design jobs. Sometimes I use them as actual bead caps to frame and protect a pretty lampworked bead. Other times I use them as spacers in a strung piece or to form the base of a riveted stack. Sometimes I form very large bead caps to use as nests in a sculptural piece. I normally make and fire my bead caps flat, rather than forming or firing them directly onto a bead, or trying to preserve their shape on a round form. Flat is easy, flat always works in the kiln, and you don't want to compromise the quality of the metal with a lower firing temperature, so don't be tempted to underfire your bead cap on a glass bead unless your design demands it.

01 | Roll a sheet of metal clay no deeper than 2 cards thick and texture as desired. **NOTE** *Thicker bead caps are very difficult to dap without breaking them. If your design demands thickness beyond 2 cards, you should form your bead cap into shape when wet, allow to dry in the desired curve, and fire it nestled in vermiculite.*

02 | Cut flat circles or other shapes in any diameter and gently smooth the edges of your cuts.

03 | Use a cocktail straw to make a small hole in the middle of the disk; be sure to remove and use or save the scrap clay from the straw. If you prefer to drill your bead caps after firing, save time at the bench by using a bead awl, toothpick, or point of a burnisher to make a pilot divot for your drill bit. Bead caps can be embellished in any way for visual interest: by piercing when the clay is fresh and wet, or by applying appliqué once the clay is leather-hard or bone-dry.

04 | Let the disks dry completely.

05 | Fire the disks flat on a kiln shelf for a full 2 hours at 1650° F (899° C). Once fired, the disks will be dead soft, which is exactly what you want for dapping, so don't hammer or tumble them until they are shaped.

06 | Place one of the fired disks into a divot in the dapping block. If you aren't sure which divot will form the correct curvature for your bead, find the perfect dap by moving the bead around the block until you find a companionable curve.

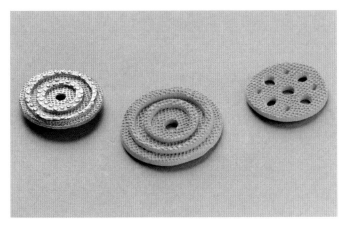

Small bead caps, one fired (left) and two greenware. I dap these after firing to form whatever curve I like.

Above, a metal dap block, a wood dap block, and three daps. Use a hammer that you don't mind marring to strike the hard steel daps, not your bench hammer.

A perforated bead cap being dapped.

Choose that divot to form your bead cap and the cap will fit the bead perfectly.

07 | Set a ball-end dapping peg on top of the disk and strike the butt end of the peg with a hammer. The force of the blow curves the flat disk down into the divot and up around the dap, making a domed piece in one simple move. If you want your cap to form an extreme curve, you may have to dap it in several steps, moving from a more gradual curve in the dapping block to a deeper one. If your bead cap is thick, you may wish to stop and anneal your bead in between daps by heating it with a torch until it glows pink. **NOTE** *Underfired or short-fired disks will simply break if you attempt to dap them; this is an excellent demonstration of why 2 hours at full temperature is vastly different than shorter or lower temperature firings.*

TIP | HOMEMADE DAPPING SET

If you don't have access to a dapping set, you can make your own low-tech version by pounding various-sized steel marbles into a soft pine 2x4. When you remove the marbles, a round depression will be left behind in the wood. Place a disk in the depression and use the round end of a hammer, or a hammer on top of the steel marble, to form the disk into a domed cap.

04
head pins

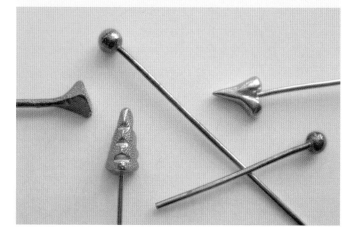

MATERIALS
Fine silver metal clay
18-, 16-, or 14-gauge fine silver wire
Finished fine silver rings (optional)

TOOLS
Flush cutters
Tumbler + mixed stainless
    steel shot
Nylon-jaw pliers

A HEAD PIN is a length of wire, generally about 1"–4" (2.5 to 10.2 cm), with a nail head, decorative ball, or sculptural end. Head pins are used for holding a bead or drilled stone in place for a dangle or moving part in a piece of finished jewelry, but sometimes, if they are sculptural, they're lovely on their own.

01 | Cut a piece of wire as long as you'd like, plus at least ¼" (6 mm) for embedding; set aside.

02 | Manipulate a bit of metal clay into a shape that pleases you and slide the wire into the shape. Embed the wire as far as practical, but at least ¼" (6 mm). Do not handle the embed after it's inserted other than to lay it on your drying surface. Any manipulation of the wire in the hole before firing can open it up and prevent it from bonding in the kiln. Make several head pins with different ends, using different wire gauges for the embeds.

03 | Let the head pins dry completely. When they are dry you should be able to pick them up by the wires without the ends wobbling because the metal clay should have shrunk around the wires as it dried. **NOTE** *If you accidentally disturb an embed and open the embed hole enough that the wire will not bond in the kiln, you have two options. The first is to let the clay piece dry completely, roll a tiny snake of fresh clay, and stick it down into the hole to fill it. Re-embed your wire into the fresh clay, cleaning up the clay that squishes up out of the hole. Let it dry again completely*

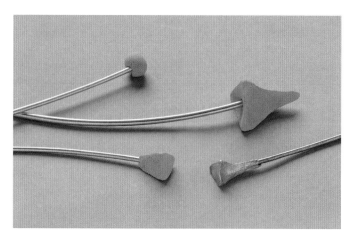

Greenware sculptural ends on fine silver wire, waiting to go into the kiln and emerge as handmade head pins, ball-end components, rivets, or sculptural one-piece earrings.

A large lotus pod head pin, detailed with a small round-end burnisher.

before firing. Second, you can replace your loosened wire with a piece of a larger gauge, one that fits tightly in the newly larger hole. Don't attempt to reset a loose wire or fill holes with slip; slip is by nature molecularly thin, so doesn't have as much silver in it as the actual clay does and won't fill gaps or holes well.

04 | Fire the head pins fully for 2 hours at 1650° F (899° C).

05 | Work-harden the wires by tumbling the head pins for several hours or overnight. Straighten the wires by holding the head pin's body with your fingers or nylon-jaw pliers and using a second nylon-jaw pliers to pull the wire straight. You can also use the metalsmithing trick of grabbing the end of the wire with flat-nose pliers and twisting the embed a quarter to a full turn. This is how ear posts and prongs are traditionally hardened, and it's quite effective, especially in combination with tumbling.

TIP | GAUGE USE FOR HEAD PINS

I usually use 18-, 16-, or 14-gauge wire for my head pins, but sometimes I make 12-gauge head pins to hang heavy lampworked beads, use as stand-alone sculptural elements, or make into prong settings for gems. When finishing these heavier-gauge head pins I usually use a simple loop connection rather than a wrapped loop and then hammer the loop for a forged finish. It's a lovely look, as you can see, and simple to achieve.

05

sculptural s-clasp

THIS BEAUTIFUL S-CLASP is made very simply, using 12-gauge wire and a bit of metal clay. In my opinion, sculptural wire embellishment like this is one of the simplest, most beautiful expressions of metal clay on a professional bench. Being able to treat your wire ends to any shape and texture you desire is amazing. And unlike any method of accomplishing this using traditional metalsmithing techniques, metal clay embellishments can be accomplished in just a few minutes. (I'm not counting the two hours in the kiln, but heck, you can be floating in the pool while that happens, vacationing on the time that you would previously have spent carving a wax blank or manually texturing a melted and forged piece.) **NOTE** *Sterling silver wire can be decorated this way as well; just drop your firing temperature down to 1200° F (649° C) to protect the wire.*

01 | Cut 3" (7.6 cm) of wire.

02 | Sculpt and press a small metal clay shape onto one end of the wire. Texture the clay as desired.

03 | Let the piece dry completely, then fire for a full 2 hours at 1650° F (899° C), or, if you chose sterling wire, fire at 1200° F (649° C) for 1 hour.

04 | Use the Wrap and Tap tool or round-nose pliers to form the wire into an S shape.

05 | Forge the wire with a chasing hammer, if desired, or simply hammer to work-harden. Brush, tumble, and patina to taste.

MATERIALS

12-gauge fine or sterling silver wire

Fine silver metal clay

TOOLS

Flush cutters

Texture sheet or rubber stamp

Wrap + Tap tool or heavy-duty round-nose pliers

Hammer

Anvil

Brass brush, tumbler + mixed stainless steel shot, patina (optional)

06
charms

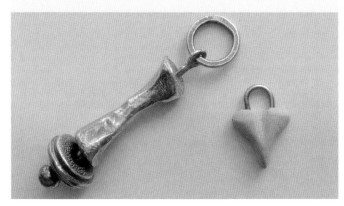

MATERIALS

Fine silver metal clay

18-, 16-, or 14-gauge fine silver wire

Small finished fine silver
  rings (optional)

TOOLS

Round-nose pliers

Flush cutters

Tumbler + mixed stainless steel shot

Patina solution (optional)

Hammer

Anvil

CHARMS can be used for anything: earrings, stringing components, little plumb bobs on the tips of pendants, ornaments on
chain links or key rings, or on a traditional charm bracelet.

01 | Use round-nose pliers to bend several ½" (13 mm) pieces
of 18-gauge wire into neat long-legged U shapes. Set aside.

02 | Roll several smooth balls of metal clay and form them
into the desired sculptural shapes.

03 | Embed the U-shaped wire bails into the metal clay
sculptures at least ⅛" (3 mm) deep. If you have small fine
silver rings handy, you can slip them onto the U-shaped wire
bails before embedding them so that in one neat step you've
got both a bail and a connection ring.

04 | Fire the charms fully, for 2 hours at 1650° F (899° C).

05 | Tumble the charms for several hours or overnight. Work-
harden the U-shaped bails by tapping them on each side with
a hammer against an anvil. Patina to taste, if desired.

TIP | CONNECTING ELEMENTS

You can also use short pieces of wire to
connect small fresh clay elements. I connected
this little Egg Clutch with tiny (⅜" [9 mm]) cuts
of 18-gauge fine silver wire. Let your pieces dry
completely, then fire them fully.

07
branches

MATERIALS
Fine silver metal clay
Fine silver metal clay slip (optional)
18-, 16- or 14-, and 12-gauge
  fine silver wire

TOOLS
Flush cutters
Round-nose pliers
Small, soft paint brush (optional)
Hammer
Anvil
Tumbler + mixed stainless steel shot
Brass brush + patina solution (optional)

WHILE ROLLED CYLINDERS (see *Snakes*, page 22) are a staple of traditional clay work, they aren't as reliable in metal clay when making large or long bars because even with proper firing, metal clay simply isn't dense enough for duty as a long, structural element like the branch shown here. Happily, though, the metal clay's shrinkage from drying

and firing allows it to permanently bond around not only embedded wires and ring shanks, but armatures and wire cores as well. This allows you to make sturdy cylindrical shapes in many sizes, including very large toggle bars, structural bars, and branches.

01 | Cut a length of 12-gauge fine silver wire to the length that you want your branch to be; set aside. This will serve as the branch's core. If you plan on connecting the branch to a chain or other strung piece, you may want to form simple loops at each end of the wire to use as connection points.

02 | Cut a piece of 16- or 14-gauge wire about 4" (10.2 cm) long. Wrap it tightly 2 or 3 times around the base wire, leaving as much of the ends sticking out as you enjoy, to create branches. These branches can be solely decorative or can serve as hanging loops or rivet posts (page 50). If you're forming a rivet post, use at least 14-gauge wire. Repeat to form two or three branches along the base wire.

03 | Cover the wire armature in metal clay by pressing bits of clay or wrapping thin, textured, rolled sheets of clay snugly around the wires. You can leave the branch wires bare or cover them with metal clay, if it suits your design. If you want to use the branch tips as resin or rivet posts, I suggest leaving them bare. If you want to hammer and pierce the ends for hanging loops, consider spearing each tip with a smoothly rolled ball of metal clay. If you do this, don't disturb the speared balls while they are drying on the tips of the wire. Like any embed, the success of the piece will depend on your careful handling when it is fresh and wet.

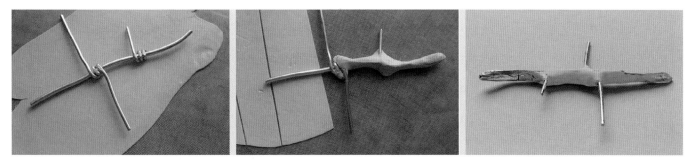

It's easy to cover a wire armature in freshly rolled fine silver metal clay. Roll the sheet thinly, and cut it into strips that you roll and form around the armature, building up the layers as necessary to create the look you want.

04 | Let the branch dry completely.

05 | **OPTIONAL** Use a small, soft paintbrush to coat the armature in several layers of slip, allowing the piece to dry completely in between coats. This technique is not structural (painting with slip doesn't fill cracks, for instance), but gives the branch a natural texture and finish that is soft and deep after firing. This is, in my opinion, one of the nicest uses for metal clay slip—creating a soft surface finish. If you slip-coat your piece, let the branch dry thoroughly again before firing.

06 | Fire the branch fully for 2 hours at 1650° F (899° C).

07 | Once cooled, you can hammer or forge the connection loops or end balls against an anvil to strengthen and add character or to provide paddles for piercing. Brush, patina, and tumble to taste.

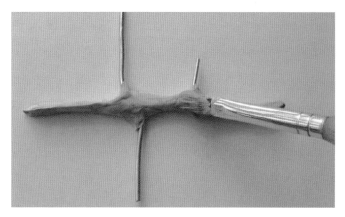

If you wish, coat the clay-covered branch with slip, for a more porous surface.

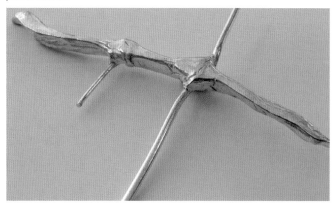

08
simple
rivet posts

MATERIALS
Fine silver metal clay
14- or 12-gauge fine silver wire

TOOLS
Flush cutters

RIVET POSTS can be set into almost any type of design and are integral in the construction of spinny rings and hinge-less boxes. In traditional bench jewelry, rivets and ear posts are soldered onto a surface that has a small divot drilled part-way into it; the divot holds the post upright for soldering. This is a technique that takes time and practice to master, and I know few metalsmiths who look forward to post-soldering. Placing a rivet post in metal clay, however, is a simple job, and comes in handy for many applications.

01 | Cut 14- or 12-gauge wire ¼"–½" (6–13 mm) longer than your desired finished post height. If you are new to riveting, give yourself the extra length. Set aside.

02 | Use fresh wet clay to form your desired shape. If you're setting your post in a ring, the sturdiest way to make the ring base is to cut it cleanly out of a thickly rolled sheet of clay be-tween 8 and 12 cards thick. Texturing the sheet before cutting adds both compression and interest to the work.

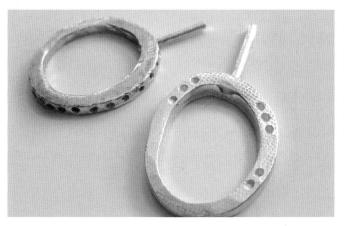

Above, fired **RIVET POST RINGS**, awaiting their embellishments. Below, a **RIVET POST RING** holding a large dapped bead cap, a smaller inverted beadcap, and a little pewter bird from Green Girl Studios makes a whimsical **BIRDBATH RING**.

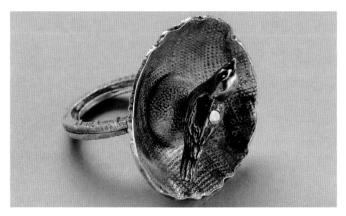

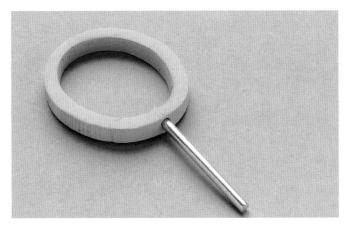

Above, a greenware **RIVET POST RING**, awaiting firing. Do not handle your embeds after they are placed. Let them dry on a kiln shelf, and move the shelf to the kiln.

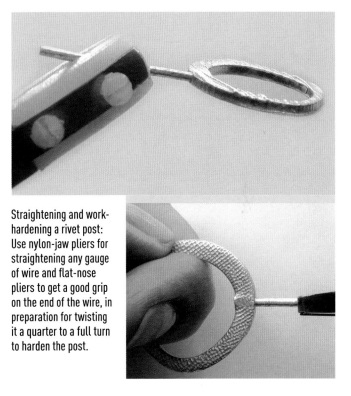

Straightening and work-hardening a rivet post: Use nylon-jaw pliers for straightening any gauge of wire and flat-nose pliers to get a good grip on the end of the wire, in preparation for twisting it a quarter to a full turn to harden the post.

03 | Push the wire into the fresh wet clay as far as possible, but at least ⅛" (3 mm). I generally push my structural embeds all the way to the opposite edge of the piece, sometimes letting them bump out a tiny bit along the inside edge of a piece like a ring.

04 | Let the piece dry without disturbing the embed. If you accidentally bump the piece and enlarge your embed hole, remove the wire, and let the piece dry completely. Fill the hole with fresh clay, re-embed your rivet post, and let the piece dry again.

05 | Fire the piece fully for 2 hours at 1650° F (899° C). Assuming you let your piece dry thoroughly and didn't disturb it after embedding the wire, the embed will permanently bond to the metal clay in the kiln. Your posts become part of the piece, not pieces stuck together with another metal, as in soldering. You don't need to drill, clean, flux, or solder your embedded posts.

06 | Work-harden the wire by tumbling the piece for several hours or overnight. Straighten the post with nylon-jaw pliers, then grab the end of the wire with flat-nose pliers, hold the ring firmly in your fingers, and pull hard on the wire end, twisting the wire a quarter to a full turn. This will harden your rivet post delightfully. This is also how ear posts and prongs are work-hardened.

09
metal clay ring bands

MATERIAL

Fine silver metal clay

TOOLS

Working surface
Roller
Firm rolling guides
Texture sheets or rubber stamps

Flexible tissue blade or thin art blade
Flush cutters
Metal ring mandrel or Wrap + Tap tool
Heavy flat- or round-nose pliers
Hammer
Anvil

I MAKE TWO different kinds of ring bands: flat strap bands, meant for forming and embedding after they are fired, and wire ring bands, which are ready to embed in fresh clay as soon as they are formed. If you're making large or heavy rings, you may prefer the comfort of a wide strap band, or you may wish to embed two wire ring bands instead of one.

01 | Roll and texture a sheet of clay, finishing with a thickness of 4 to 6 cards if this is your first time making and bending a strap band for embedding. If you're a pro, you can make bands up to 12 cards thick. If you want your finished band to be thicker than that, you should probably form and fire it into your desired curvature instead of planning on bending it around a mandrel after firing. There's a limit to what thickness of metal clay can be dapped and bent without breaking. Use firm rolling guides to make sure your finished product is perfectly even and nicely compressed. Since you'll be bending the metal after it's fired, it's important to begin with sheets of clay that aren't too thick. Thicker bands are delightful and longer-wearing, but take strength and confidence to bend. If your band is 6 cards or thicker after firing, you might have to stop several times during the bending process to anneal the band in order to bend it.

02 | Cut a 2½"–3½" (6.4–8.9 cm) strap out of the sheet in any width you'd like for your ring, keeping in mind that the clay will shrink at least 10% in any direction. Most people are not comfortable with ring shanks that are wider than ½" (1.3 cm), so keep that in mind while you're cutting. It's worth noting here that every design choice you make, including thickness, texture, and whether or not there are appliquéd ornaments or cut holes, can change the fired, finished dimensions of your ring. I can tell you that the total overall shrinkage of your band will be about 15%, but it's impossible to say, "For a size 7 ring, cut your band exactly 3" (7.5 cm) long." (Even though it's close to that.) In general, most finished ring sizes of 5–8 come from fresh clay strips cut between 2½"–3" (6.4–7.6 cm) long. My best band sizing advice to you is to make it ¼" (6 mm) longer than you think you'll need it. You can always trim off the excess after firing and forming—a relatively minor waste to assure you of a perfect size every time.

03 | Ornament, appliqué, or pierce the freshly cut ring band to taste. If you cut holes in your band, be sure to not make them too close to any edge, and try not to place holes at the exact center point of the ring, as this is where most of the force of the bend will be concentrated.

04 | Let the band dry flat.

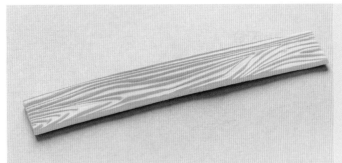

Above, a greenware **STRAP BAND RING SHANK**, ready to fire flat in the kiln. After firing, it will be bent around a ring mandrel, trimmed to size with flush cutters, and given pretty little embed legs. Then it will be embedded in a fresh wet fine silver metal clay pad and refired to create a ring band made exactly to size.

TIP | BAND SHAPE

You can make ring bands out of metal clay or fine silver wire in any shape you like, but I prefer oval or squared-off ring bands because they're easier to fit to real human fingers. With a round band, you have only one option for fitting: get it over your knuckle. But most of our fingers are wider at the knuckles than at the base of our fingers where we wear our rings, so a round ring that fits over the knuckle may flop around up on top of the finger. This is okay for a plain flat ring band, but if you've added a bit of excitement on top, like a skyscraper or spinner, flopping is the last thing you want. When you form a ring band into an oval, you allow the ring the option to fit snugly at the base of the finger so that the ring top doesn't flop.

How does this work? Happily, your knuckle joints are wider than they are tall, so if you make an oval ring band, you can turn it sideways to put it on, slipping it over the flat of your knuckle, then turn it right side up for a neat fit without a lot of play. I'm not sure why more ring bands aren't crafted to be oval, because it's such a natural solution to the problem many people have fitting rings.

Left: Fired Strap Band Ring Shanks right out of the kiln, and bent and formed around a ring mandrel. Note the turned up leg ends, suitable for embedding. *Middle:* Forming the band carefully around a steel sizing mandrel. *Right:* annealing the band with a torch flame to soften it, and allow it to continue bending around the mandrel without breaking. You may have to anneal very thick bands a couple of times during the bending process to avoid stressing the metal.

05 | Fire the band fully for 2 hours at 1650° F (899° C). Full firing is crucial for the success of any piece that will be formed or forged, and ring bands are a wonderful illustration for the difference a full firing makes. Underfired or short-fired bands will simply break, or embeds will pop out, if you attempt to form them or size them up on a mandrel.

06 | After firing, quench or cool the ring bands and use your fingers to bend the band to size around a marked steel ring mandrel. Be certain to support the band firmly in the center, against the mandrel, as you are bending; if you don't, it will want to form a "V" shape and may snap in the middle. Also, as I mentioned previously, if you short-fired or underfired the band, you won't be able to form or forge it successfully. To size a wide band, place the center of the wide strap on the mark for the size you want. Choose a size that's at least half, perhaps as much as two, sizes too small. This will allow you room to size up the band during work-hardening. **NOTE** *One of the most delightful ways to work-harden a strap band is to hammer it around a steel mandrel, but this always has the effect of enlarging the band. If you know that you want a lot of hammer texture on the outside, make the band smaller by as much as two sizes. If you have texture that you want to preserve, you will probably just want to tap it with a leather or rubber mallet, or lightly with a chasing hammer, and it will only enlarge a half size.*

Temporarily work-hardening a formed ring shank. I do this only to stabilize ring shanks on my bench while they are waiting to be used; the bands will anneal in a full firing and will require a final work-hardening before use.

Left: A fired, bent and sized strap band ring, with appliquéd and textured stabilizing strips, neatly embedded in a fresh clay pad. When the pad is dry, I will wet it, and squidge a bone-dry building or other focal onto the pad. *Middle:* The shank of this ring is nestled in vermiculite for firing. The entire clay pot will go into the kiln. *Right:* This ring can also be fired upside down, on the kiln shelf. Choose your firing position based on common sense; what will protect your piece the best?

Make the bend cleanly and carefully around the mandrel; if you just grab the ends and pull the metal around the mandrel, the band will form the dreaded "V" shape and break in the middle. If the band was made thicker than 3 or 4 cards, you may need to stop bending at several points in the process, anneal, and then quench the piece. (See *Annealing*, page 133, and both the ring-bending and annealing demonstrations on the enclosed DVD.)

07 | Use pliers to slightly bend the legs of the band so they are suitable for embedding. Your band may end up round, with little straight feet; oval, with curved embed legs; or horseshoe shaped. As long as you can cleanly embed it into a fresh metal clay pad, any shape you enjoy will work.

08 | Use sharp flush cutters to trim the band length to size.

09 | Use your fingers to adjust the shape and size of the band. If you won't be embedding this piece into a pad immediately, you might want to work-harden it a bit so it doesn't get bent up on your bench or in your toolbox.

A WAVE RING, ready to fire. It can be supported in vermiculite or fired between two kiln posts. Because it is uneven, it cannot fire upside down on a shelf.

10 | Embed the band ends into a prepared fresh wet clay pad. As with all structural embeds, push your tips in as deeply as is practical. The depth of the pad is a common-sense decision—very thin pads are a poor choice, since the pad is all that's supporting your embedded band. I usually make my fresh clay pads a minimum finished thickness of 4 cards. If there are other embeds going into the top of the same pad, as in a more advanced piece that contains rivet posts or prongs on top, then I make the pad 6 to 8 cards thick. Embeds can technically be done into thin pads, but they will never be as sturdy or long-wearing as those done into a thicker layer of metal.

11 | If you plan to use your shank and pad as a solder base, let it dry and fire it fully for 2 hours at 1650° F (899° C). If you're using it as a base for other dry clay attachments such as appliquéd bezel rings for resin or stone fills, a Skyscraper Ring (page 117), or any other appliquéd

attachment or excitement, let the base dry and appliqué your greenware excitements to the ring by squidging them onto the top of the dry pad with water or thin slip. Be certain not to disrupt the embedded shank while you're embellishing the top of the pad. After the appliqué is set, let the piece re-dry, and fire it fully for another 2 hours at 1650°F (899°C). (The shank won't mind the double firing a bit; in fact, you can fire your finished metal as many times as you like. Just remember that firing means annealing, so your pieces will be dead soft again after each heating cycle.) Place the piece upside down on a kiln shelf to fire if the top of the ring is flat, or, if you have a sculptural piece, nestled in a dish of vermiculite. **NOTE** *If you wish to place rivet posts or other embeds in the top of your ring pad, you have several choices. The easiest method is to place those embeds into a second pad, let both pads and their embeds dry fully, and then squidge the two pads together with water or slip, as I did with the* Returning Ring *(page 109). If you prefer a soldered*

TIP | ONE BEAD RING

This simple and elegant ring is also made from a flat band. In this case, cut your wet clay band 1" (2.5 cm) longer than one you would embed. The extra length enables the shank sides to rise  up sculpturally along the single bead to hold it. Use a cocktail straw to cut at least one hole at each end of the band. (If you want to drill your holes after firing instead of making them in the fresh clay and you know where you want them placed, you may wish to make tiny pilot holes with a bead awl or toothpick to avoid having to start holes from scratch in the fired metal.) You'll use these holes to rivet or wirework the bead in place after you've fired and shaped it. If you're unsure about where to cut the holes in order to fit your bead, do yourself a favor and make multiple holes along the side of the band. This way you can experiment with the bead placement, plus holes save on material and weight and can be used as a design feature. Note how the cast sterling silver version above has only one hole, thereby limiting the number of beads that will work in the ring. The rings below show different shapes; a ribboned band holds a clear purple flower from my torch, and a band with three choices of hole holds a Lotus Pod bead by Dustin Tabor.

attachment, which can be longer-wearing, you can fire both pads separately with their embeds and sweat-solder the pads together after firing.

Alternatively, if you wish to use only one pad for embeds from both top and bottom, you can take advantage of the same technique used in divot-making, allowing the texture on one surface to dry before placing embedded balls in the other side. Place your ring shank in the fresh, soft pad of clay, and allow the surface with the embedded shank to dry while the underside of the pad sits against a piece of Teflon, glass, or plastic. This will keep the top side of the ring fresh and wet, while the underside, with the embedded shank, sets up.

When the side with the embedded shank is set up, gently turn the ring over, and while supporting the pad with your fingers and being careful not to disturb the embedded shank, place your secondary embeds into the top of the pad. (This is obviously a more technically difficult method, and shouldn't be attempted until you feel comfortable handling the clay in all stages of dryness and have had success making embeds.) Support the piece as it dries, either between two kiln feet or in a small clay flower pot filled with vermiculite. Both supports are practical choices, because they can be placed directly into the kiln when the ring is dry.

10
wire ring bands

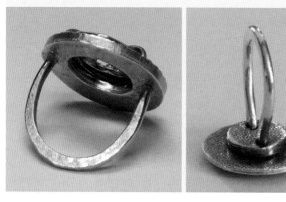

MATERIALS

14-, 12-, or 10-gauge
  fine silver wire

TOOLS

Flush cutters

Metal ring mandrel or Wrap + Tap tool

Heavy-duty round-, flat- or
  chain-nose pliers

Hammer

Anvil

Tumbler + mixed stainless steel
  shot (optional)

FINE SILVER WIRE makes a lovely ring band, too. Fine silver is softer, even after work-hardening, than most other metals, so if I'm forming shanks from wire, I generally pair two shanks of 14- or 12-gauge wire, or use a single shank of 12- or 10-gauge wire to form them. I'd discourage you from using sterling silver wire for your metal clay ring bands, since you'll have to drop the firing temperature of the finished ring to 1200°–1490° F (649°–810° C) to be certain that you will avoid damaging the sterling. However, if you want to use thinner bands

and you don't intend to form, forge, or work your finished ring, you may decide that the stronger, thinner band is worth the tradeoff. Also keep in mind that if you use sterling it will blacken and have to be cleaned after firing.

01 | Cut 2½"–3½" (6.4–8.9 cm) of wire.

02 | Use your fingers to form the wire around the mandrel, or use a Wrap + Tap tool. Make the ring ½ to 2 sizes smaller than your desired finished size to allow room for sizing up when hammering or forging around a ring mandrel after firing.

03 | Use pliers to bend the wire ends parallel, forming embed feet. When you're pleased with the size and shape of the shank, hammer or forge the wire for visual and tactile interest. Hold the wire ends in place while you forge so the shank doesn't spread open while you're hammering the base.

It's easiest to shape and work the band now when it's loose, rather than when it's embedded into a ring top. Save any hammering against the mandrel for after it's fired because finishing of that sort will change the band size. If you plan on texturing the outside of the band by hammering it against the mandrel, you should create the band so it's several sizes smaller than your desired finished size.

04 | Embed the band (or bands) into a wet clay ring base, 4 to 8 cards thick, and let the assembly dry completely.

05 | Appliqué anything you like to the top of the pad, and let the entire assembly re-dry completely.

06 | Fire fully for 2 hours at 1650° F (899° C), or drop the temperature accordingly if you use sterling wire.

Above: A collection of fine silver wire bands. You can embed one, two, or more in a pad to give you exactly the support you need.

Below: Forging a shank for sculptural interest before embedding. Be sure to support the neck of an open shank while forging or it will want to open up.

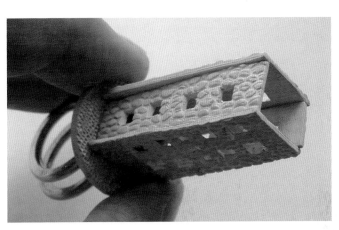

Above: A greenware building ring, ready for the kiln. I chose to use two wire shanks in this pad for greater stability when worn.

Below: work-hardening wire bands around a mandrel, after firing. This will rapidly size up a ring, so build your wire shanks at least one size smaller than your desired finished size to leave room for this essential hardening step.

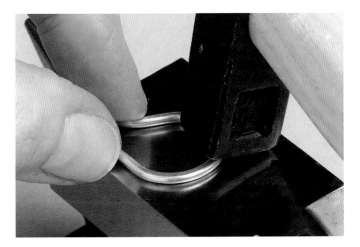

07 | Work-harden and size the band by hammering it around a ring mandrel. If desired, use a chasing hammer and stainless steel ring mandrel to texture the outside of the embedded wire ring band, sizing the ring up at the same time. Tumble as desired for finish, but don't rely on tumbling alone to work-harden the ring; you want to get it between a hammer and steel in as many ways as possible.

11
box-building

MATERIALS

Fresh fine silver metal clay

Graph paper for cutting a pattern (optional)

TOOLS

Sharp tissue blade

Soft, small paintbrush

Kiln shelf or Solderite pad

Fine sandpaper or emery board (optional)

Vermiculite + fireproof dish (optional)

Brass brush, tumbler + mixed stainless steel shot, patina (optional)

BOX-BUILDING is a term that covers any kind of 3-D pattern-piece construction. Boxes can be open circles, skyscrapers, spacer beads, or anything with space inside. Think of building circular and straight-sided boxes with metal clay as if you are making a model with thin cardboard. Generally, just a wash of water on either side of a join and some focused squidging will be sufficient to build your metal clay boxes. Slip isn't necessary for most joinery, despite being commonly used. Why make a mess if you don't have to? Because slip is simply a slurry of dry clay and water, when you put water on dry clay, you are creating your own slip exactly where needed. Keep in mind that you aren't gluing the pieces together; you're using the water or slip as an agent to make the tiny clay slabs sticky so that they grab and bond together before firing. Make your cuts cleanly so that you don't have to file and sand them later, other than for minor adjustments in your joinery.

Circle Boxes

01 | If you find it helpful, make paper patterns of the clay pieces that you will use to assemble your box in order to plan your cuts. You'll need one circle for the top, one for the bottom, and a long rectangular strip to connect the two, creating the box side. (You'll let the strip dry, on edge, into a circular shape before assembling your box.)

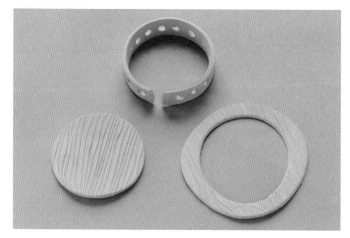

The pieces of a basic **CIRCLE BOX**, leather-hard and ready for assembly.

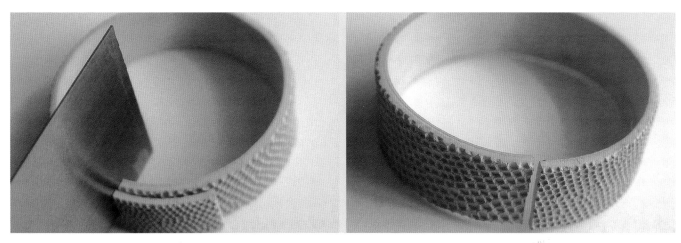

A beautiful **CIRCLE BOX** spacer, hard leather-hard, and ready to slice through at an overlap to achieve a perfect butt joint. Joins cut this cleanly will only require a small wash of water to squidge them together. You can skip the slip and achieve a perfect join that preserves every dot of your texture. Alternatively, you can take advantage of the gap to slip in a bail (see Tip below).

02 | Roll and texture the metal clay to a finished size of 2 to 4 cards thick. Boxes tend to hold their shape, so they don't require thick slab construction.

03 | Use the paper patterns as templates to cut out the top and bottom shapes, or use cookie cutters. I made the two circle boxes shown here by using my Matfer 1³/₁₆" (30 mm) pastry cutter for the exterior diameter and a 1" (25 mm) circle cutter for the interior of each top piece.

04 | Ornament the flat strip spacer with holes or cutwork immediately after it is cut. Move very quickly with this task, because you'll need to shape the strip into a circle and you don't want it to become too dry to bend. If you plan on adding appliqué (page 24), do it after the box is assembled and bone-dry. My spacer strip was cut with a tissue blade, to about 3" (7.6 cm) long, and allowed to dry, overlapped, inside one of the plastic cups I use to store my fresh clay. **NOTE** *Letting your*

TIP | ADDING A BAIL

You can take advantage of the gap in your circle spacer and insert a dry clay bail. Simply cut a U-shaped piece of clay that fits perfectly into the gap. Let the bail become bone-dry, add a hanging ring onto it if desired, and slip the bail into place in the gap with a bit of water and squidging after the ring is set on the base. After the base, ring, and bail set up, attach the top of the box with more water and more squidging, and the structure will hold the bail in place.

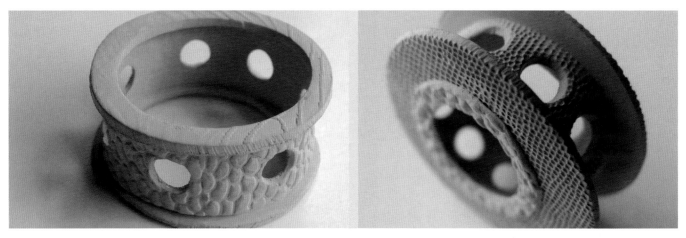

Greenware circle boxes, assembled and ready for firing. Left, a **FIRST KISS PIPE RING**, right, a round open bead.

strips dry in an overlap allows you to cut down through both layers at once with a tissue blade, ensuring a perfect match, and join strap bands without slip joints.

It's easiest to dry the circular strip supported on the inside of a form (rather than the outside) because the clay shrinks when it dries and can be difficult to remove from around the outside of a form. Alternatively, if the clay strip is thick enough to hold its own form, you can just dry it on the tabletop. I use small, clean kiln shelves as drying pads; they're quite convenient and, as the name implies, can go right into the kiln.

05 | If desired, trim the circular strip once it's hard leather-hard to bone-dry for a perfect beveled butt joint. If you plan on doing this, cut your initial wet clay strip a little longer than necessary to form a ring and allow it to overlap as it dries. When you're ready to cut, position a thin, sharp, flexible tissue blade above the ring and slice straight down through both layers at once. This assures a perfectly

matched cut and a seam that can be easily joined without slip.

06 | Add a wash of water on each cut end, and then squidge the ends to form a clean bond. Let the join dry. If necessary, erase any evidence of the join with a damp paintbrush. This is a much easier method than using slip to join the band. Glued slip joins will always need cleanup, either by carving or filing; they generate waste, dust, and mess, and, because

TIP | TURNING CIRCLE BOXES INTO RINGS

FIRST KISS PIPE RINGS are basically circle boxes. I used beveled butt joints to connect the ends of the flat strip for a perfectly clean, strong bond. I strengthened the rings even more when I added the bone-dry top and bottom cut-out circles.

they are more porous, they will never be as strong a bond as a clay body-to-clay body join.

07 | Set the pattern pieces on a kiln shelf or Solderite pad and let them become hard leather-hard to bone-dry, carefully flipping them several times (if necessary) during the drying process to prevent warping.

08 | To assemble the box, squidge the spacer strip onto the box's bottom using a thin wash of water or slip. Once it's set up, do the same to attach the top. You may wish to lightly rub the edge of your bone-dry spacer against a piece of fine sandpaper to even it out before attaching. Be fairly assertive about your squidging. Let the assembled box dry completely.

09 | Fire fully for 2 hours at 1650° F (899° C). If your box has a flat top or bottom, you can fire it sitting on the kiln shelf. If it's sculptural or delicate, fire it nestled in a dish of vermiculite. Brush, tumble, and patina to taste.

Straight-Side Boxes

01 | If you wish, make paper patterns of the clay pieces that will make up your box in order to plan your cuts. You'll need 3 or more evenly sized rectangles or squares for the sides and, if you wish, a top and/or bottom. At least one joining pad, either a top or a bottom, will add stability to your piece.

02 | Roll and texture the metal clay to a finished thickness of 2 to 4 cards. If your box will have a top and a bottom, you can make the sides thinner.

Small box forms: a little building and an open birdhouse.

03 | Use the paper patterns as templates to cut out the shapes, or use a tissue blade to make freehand cuts.

04 | As with the Circle Boxes (page 60), if you wish to embellish your box with windows or holes, you'll need to make these cuts while the clay is fresh and wet.

05 | Set the pattern pieces on a kiln shelf or Solderite pad and let them become hard leather-hard to bone-dry, flipping them several times during the drying process to prevent warping.

06 | Assemble the pieces, squidging them together using a thin wash of water and slip. The moment of attachment should be chosen by the difficulty of the assembly. There are times you might need the clay to be a bit more flexible in order to get a clean build, so in that case, leather-hard would be easier than bone-dry, but you will always have the best success box-building if you wait to assemble until your pieces are dry. You may wish to rub the sides of the pieces lightly against an emery board or a piece of fine sandpaper to

be sure that they are straight and true. **NOTE** *A fresh clay roof can either dry on a form before attachment or can be supported with a drinking straw if it goes on leather-hard.*

07 | If you need to strengthen or fill a joint after construction, don't use slip to fill cracks, gaps, or joins. Instead, let the fully assembled piece dry completely. Roll a tiny thin snake of fresh clay (see *Snakes*, page 22), then wet the join with a thin wash of water or slip and press and burnish the freshly rolled snake into the crevice or gap. This technique is frequently used in traditional clay work but rarely needed, except for cosmetic fixes, at the small scale most people work in metal clay.

08 | Fire fully, for 2 hours at 1650° F (899° C), either standing up on a kiln shelf, or, if your piece is delicate or sculptural, nestled in a dish of vermiculite. After firing, brush, patina, and tumble to taste.

A straight-sided building being assembled, one wall at a time. If you choose to set your roof while it is still leather-hard to use that flexibility in joining, it can be supported with a drinking straw while it dries completely.

12
prongs

MATERIALS

Fresh fine silver metal clay base

18-, 16-, or 14-gauge fine silver wire

TOOLS

Flush cutters

Metal files

Tweezers

Vermiculite + fire-proof dish

PRONGS are used to hold stones, beads, or other materials in place in finished jewelry. Setting prongs is quite similar to setting posts; in traditional bench work, each prong is soldered onto a base or into a crown shape with other prongs, and then attached to the base. If you're willing to use fine silver wire for your settings, placing prongs in metal clay is as simple as embedding and fully firing them. Sterling wire can be substituted, of course, if you're willing to compromise the quality of your metal clay setting by underfiring in favor of a thinner, stronger wire.

01 | Cut the wire into 2 or more ¾" (1.9 cm) pieces. Finish one end of each wire with either a beveled flush cut or decoratively balled ends (see *Drawing a bead*, page 67). Set aside.

02 | Cut a fresh metal clay piece in a shape suitable for your base. This can be for a ring, pendant, or other component.

03 | Embed the prongs into the base in an arrangement that is roughly 10–15% wider than you'll need for setting the stone or other item. The unpredictable shrinkage of the clay can make estimating the finished spread of your prongs difficult. Some pieces shrink in height more than diameter; some do the opposite. Sometimes you have to try several times before you have a perfect setting for a stone. Happily, your unused prong settings for one design can be employed holding other stones, felt balls, beach glass, found objects, vintage Monopoly pieces, or anything else you can think of. You can make your prongs short

TIP | **SIZING YOUR SETTINGS**

If you want to make prong settings that are sized to fit a stone and can be embedded in your metal clay work, cut your prongs a few millimeters longer than necessary and push them all the way through their pad. Let the assembly dry fully, then fire, nestled in vermiculite. After firing, tumble the prong setting for several hours or overnight. The portions of the prongs that stick out of the bottom of the setting can be used as embeds in another fresh pad of clay. This will allow you to assure the finished size of the setting before it's fired into your piece, as an already fired setting will not shrink again in a second firing.

Two **CAGE SETTINGS** waiting for their treasures. One has been patinated with liver of sulphur (far left) and then tumbled; one has simply been tumbled.

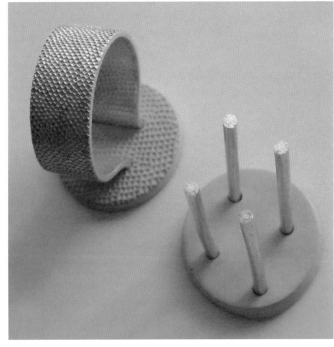

A CAGE SETTING assembly drying in two stages; one pad holds the ring shank, one pad holds four large, heavy-gauge prongs. The ring will be assembled bone-dry, with a wash of water between the pads, and these prongs will be cut to size and beveled after firing.

and notched to grab the table of a cut stone or long and tendrilled to wrap decoratively around a cabochon or odd-shaped object. You can have as few as two prongs or as many as will fit. If you prefer a traditional fine jewelry setting, you can always buy one in fine silver or gold and embed it into your clay before firing.

04 | Let the piece dry fully.

05 | Appliqué the pad with your prongs to any other component you like before firing. For instance, you could attach a pad with a cage setting to a dry pad with a ring band already embedded. Since both pads are dry, you can simply attach them with a small wash of water or slip, squidge them together, and let the entire assembly dry.

06 | Fire fully, for 2 hours at 1650° F (899° C). Support pieces like this nestled in a ceramic or steel dish filled with vermiculite.

13
drawing a bead

MATERIALS
Fine silver wire in any gauge

TOOLS
Protective tweezers or Third Hand
Torch
Kiln brick

Wide-mouthed glass, ceramic, or stainless steel bowl filled with cool water, deep enough to submerge not only your hot wire, but the ends of your tweezers or Third Hand as well.
Rimmed metal cookie sheet (optional)
Metal hole punch or drill (optional)
Tumbler + mixed stainless steel shot

THIS METALSMITHING technique will come in very handy in your metal clay work. Drawing a bead is a skill that will allow you to make your own head pins, certainly, but can be used for decorative embedded prongs, hammered and pierced mechanisms, or any time you would like to use a

wire but soften the end. The term "drawing a bead" is metalsmithing lingo for using fire to draw the molten end of the wire into a ball, or "bead."

01 | Cut 2" (5.1 cm) or more of wire. If you want a shorter head pin, don't work with shorter wire; instead, cut it down after beading. **NOTE** *For your own safety, don't use fire on loose pieces of wire shorter than 2" (5.1 cm). They are too easy to lose or drop, and one tiny piece of red-hot wire can start a fire or severely burn you.*

02 | Place the water-filled bowl next to the kiln brick. If you're working on a wooden tabletop or if you're just learning to work with fire, you may want to place all of these items on a rimmed metal cookie sheet for extra protection.

03 | Use tweezers to hold the wire directly over the water-filled bowl. This is very important for your safety! As you're learning to do this technique, you may have molten balls

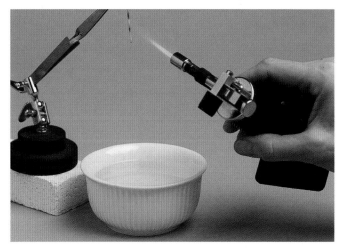

Warm the wire with your flame before you attempt to draw the bead.

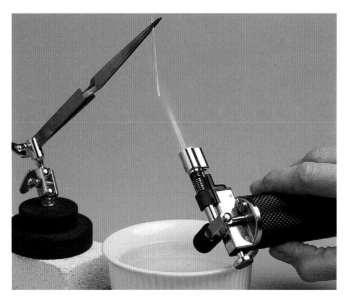

When your wire is warm, move your torch flame below the wire, and use the tip of the cone of your flame to heat the very end of the wire.

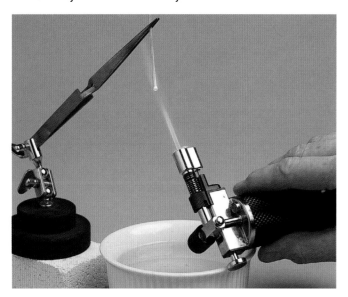

The wire tip will become red hot and begin to bead. Remove your flame when the bead starts to dance.

melt off of the end of the wire and fall, so if you're over water, the quench bowl will catch them instead of your workbench, leg, or carpet.

04 | Position the wire high enough so you have room underneath it for the torch. I often place the base of my Third Hand on a riser for this job. If you want the ball to be perfectly centered on the wire, keep in mind that you need to hold the wire straight up and down. Gravity is your friend, as long as you remember that it exists.

05 | Turn on the torch and warm the wire for at least 1" (2.5 cm) above the spot you'd like to form the ball. When the wire is warm, but not red-hot, turn your torch so the tip of the cone of the flame directly heats the warmed wire tip. There will be a flare off the wire end if your flame is correctly positioned, and a ball of molten metal will rapidly form. If the ball doesn't form, your torch isn't hot enough, you're not holding the tip of the flame's cone exactly on the wire tip, or you aren't pointing the flame tip upward.

TIP | PETAL ENDS

You can make petal-shaped ball-ends by drawing the bead flat on a kiln brick instead of suspended in the air. The bead will dance up the wire, and you can chase it with the tip of the flame cone until you're pleased with the shape. If you want a very large bead, take your flame away and let the wire and bead cool periodically as you move it up the brick.

06 | The gathering ball of molten metal will grow quickly and reach a point that it dances on the wire end. When you see the molten ball begin to dance, immediately remove the wire from the flame to allow the molten ball to cool. If you continue to heat the dancing ball without letting it set, the ball will drop off, potentially burning you or starting a fire. Drawing beads over a quench bowl is essential, even for experienced metalsmiths; sometimes there are weak points or flaws in a draw of wire that you can't see, which can result in unexpected separation of the molten end. Quench the entire wire and the tweezers or Third Hand tips (which will have become very hot) in the bowl of cool water.

07 | To form a larger bead or metal ball, rewarm the wire shank and point the tip of the cone of the flame upward again, directly on the balled wire tip. There will be another flare off of the wire end. Continue heating and enlarging the molten end of the wire only until the ball dances again, then immediately remove the flame.

08 | Once you're satisfied with your drawn bead, quench the assembly, including the tweezers or Third Hand tips. If you require a still-larger ball, you're best off making it flat on a brick or adding it with a rolled ball of metal clay and firing it in the kiln. There's a limit to how much wire can bead while suspended in the air.

09 | Leave the resultant ball, or "bead," on the end of the wire as is, or forge it with a hammer and pierce it with a metal hole punch or drill for a jump ring or a fused, soldered, or riveted connection.

14
fused wire chain

MATERIALS
16-, 14- or 12-gauge fine silver wire

Kiln brick
Torch
Protective tweezers
Bowl of water
Rimmed metal cookie sheet (optional)
Chasing hammer
Anvil

TOOLS
Dowel or Wrap + Tap tool
Flush cutters
Two pairs of flat- or chain-nose pliers

MAKING CHAIN is one of the real pleasures of the bench for me, and it's fairly easy to do by fusing fine silver wire rings. For this technique, you'll set already closed rings into a channel carved into a soft kiln brick, while you fuse the ring connecting them. This way you never have to bother with holding the assembly with tweezers or clamps while you fuse. This technique is not suitable for most soldering jobs, because the solder flows to the base of a joint, and relies on a completely clean and fluxed surface. The dust from the soft kiln brick would make a mess of the fluxed surface and might be caught by the solder flow as it is drawn into the joint. Fusing, however, relies on flowing the top surface of the joint of a pure metal ring, so doesn't drag any molten material along the bottom of the brick.

Jump rings cut from 14-gauge fine silver wire.

01 | Wrap the wire around the dowel for as many revolutions as you need rings, plus a few more, to make a neat, tight coil.

02 | Flush-cut the rings from the coil. Be sure to use good-quality cutters for this job, because precise and evenly matched cuts are crucial for the next steps. Most cutters cut flush on only one side, so you will need to flip your cutter over between cuts, to make a flush cut on each side of the ring. You'll also need to be able to see the cuts and joins clearly, so wear magnifiers if necessary, and work in good light. Poorly cut rings simply cannot be fused or soldered; there is no fix for a badly made joint.

03 | Use two chain-nose pliers to neatly close 1 jump ring and place it on the kiln brick. You may wish to set your brick and quench bowl on a rimmed metal cookie sheet for safety.

04 | Use the torch to either warm the whole ring slowly or focus the flame on the kiln brick in front of the jump ring's

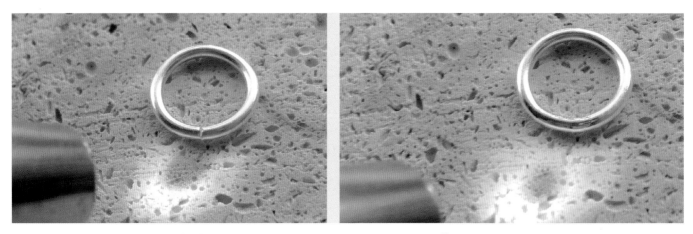

For an easy fuse, simply heat the kiln brick in front of the join. This is easy to do correctly as you can just "light up" the brick, by making it red hot. The ring will evenly heat and fuse on its own, only at the join.

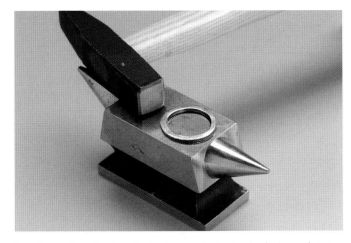

I use the chasing side of my riveting hammer for forging, hardening, and most general-purpose hammering.

Plain rings look beautiful with light forging.

joint. Either method works well, but the latter will keep the surface of the ring more pristine, as it tends to only flow the join. If you use your flame on the entire surface of the ring, you risk flowing the whole surface of the ring. You may or may not want to do this; it really depends on the look you're going for in your finished piece. A fully flowed piece will have a rougher and more porous surface, which might be to your advantage if you're creating metalwork meant to appear antique or to take on a rich patina.

05 | Once the metal at the joint flows, immediately remove the flame. If you hold the flame on the work even a second too long, the joint, which is the hottest part, will flow apart and be ruined. Learn to rotate your torch flame up and down on the kiln brick without changing your basic hand position. This will give you great control over your flame.

06 | Use protective tweezers to pick up the ring and quench it and the tweezer tips in the water-filled bowl.

07 | Use the hammer and anvil to texture the ring as desired.

08 | Repeat Steps 3 to 7 to make as many closed rings as will fill half the desired chain length. **NOTE** *Both your torch tip and kiln brick will get very hot as you work, so take care not to burn yourself on them, and train yourself to touch the water in your*

TIP | CLOSING JUMP RINGS

The easiest way to close a jump ring is to bring it slightly past the join in either direction, creating spring tension, then close it.

The kiln brick makes fused chain easy; just dig a small channel to support the two closed rings on either side of your active ring. Pile up extra links on the brick as your chain grows.

Remember to work-harden each link on a block or anvil, turning the ring so that all parts of it are hammered.

quench bowl before you pick up the quenched rings. If the water feels warm, do not touch the ring or quenched item. Change the water in the quench bowl without touching the potentially still-hot metal piece in the water.

09 | Use 1 open jump ring to connect 2 fused rings, making sure your joint is clean and tight. Place the two already fused rings vertically in a small channel dug in your kiln brick. The channel should be deep enough to support the rings, but not so deep that the ring you're fusing touches the finished rings standing on end.

10 | Fuse the new ring as if it were the only ring on your brick. Since it's not touching the other two rings, there's no danger that they will fuse together, even if you flow the entire surface of the new ring. Use tweezers to pick up the length of chain and quench. You can forge the new ring or leave as-is; it's a lovely look to alternate heavily forged and plain round links in a handmade chain.

11 | Connect the chain's end link to another fused ring with a newly added ring. Make sure your new join is clean and tight. Stand the two rings it adjoins on end in the channel, piling the extra ring or rings on the brick behind it. Fuse the new ring as before. Quench the entire chain and tweezers tips. Repeat to fuse all the rings together into a chain of your desired length.

12 | Once the chain is complete, work-harden the links by hammering them one at a time on an anvil. Be careful not to mar the neighboring links as you hammer. Work-harden a bit of the link, turn it, do some more, turn it again. You may also tumble your chain for a lovely surface polish, but only hammering or forging will fully work-harden the chain.

15
metal clay chain

MATERIALS
25–100 g of fine silver metal clay

TOOLS
Work surface

Texture sheets or rubber stamps (optional)
Sharp, thin, clean tissue blade
Soft, clean small paintbrush
Water

IT'S EASIER than you might think to make beautiful fine silver metal clay chain, fired together in the kiln. You can achieve a level of pattern, texture, and hand-finishing with metal clay that is nearly impossible at the bench, and it's easy to finger-form the links into delicate shapes while the clay is wet.

01 | Use metal clay to form enough circular or oval rings (page 36) to make half of the desired chain length. Your rings can be of any size or depth that please you, but be sure not to cut them too thin in any dimension. I tend to work with

a minimum size of 4 cards thick and $^1/_{16}$" (2 mm) wall thickness, and often significantly larger or heavier than that. **NOTE** *It's quite easy to cut round rings and gently move them into ovals or other shapes with your fingers. Oval rings are sometimes more desirable for metal clay chain links because the wedge cuts necessary for linking the rings can be placed at the ends of the ovals, and thus are better hidden with this shape. Plus, you can cover more length with the same amount of clay if your links are elongated.*

02 | Let all the links dry completely and then, if you like, pre-fire half of them. Fire them fully, for 2 hours at 1650° F (899° C), if you intend to hammer or forge them before assembling your chain. The advantages to firing half of your links in advance are several. First, you have the opportunity, if you fully fire them, to forge them before they are part of a chain. Second, your assembled chain is much easier to inspect after joining if the only cut links are the bone-dry links. If your entire assembled chain is bone-dry, it can be difficult to keep track of which links you've already inspected.

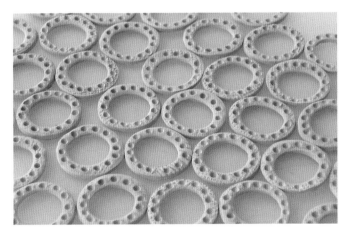

Bone-dry links, waiting to be cut to join already fired rings.

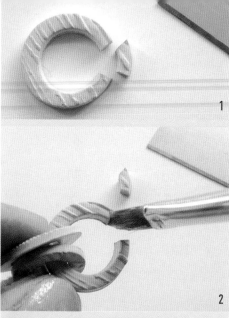

Cutting and rejoining a bone-dry link:

1. Use a sharp tissue blade to cleanly cut a keystone wedge out of the link.

2. Place two bone-dry or fired links on the cut link, and lightly wash the cut edges of the ring with water.

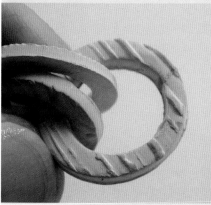

3. Slip the wedge back in (right side up!) and gently brush the damp joins with a soft paintbrush.

4. Remove excess water with the same brush, and allow the joined ring to dry before adding more links.

5. Inspect the cut ring after it is dry to see if you need to touch up your seams with a damp paintbrush or a tiny bit of sanding.

03 | Use a tissue blade to cut a small keystone wedge out of one bone-dry connecting link. Pay attention to the orientation of the wedge; it needs to be inserted into the cut link exactly the same way it came out. I actually texture both sides of my chain links differently so that I know that my wedge is going back in right side up. You really only have one shot to do this perfectly, so you don't want to waste it by having to remove and flip the wedge. You'll know if your blade isn't sharp, clean, or thin enough if your dry clay links chip as you cut them.

04 | Slide 2 closed links onto 1 open cut link. Place a very small wash of water on each end of the cut link and carefully slide the wedge-shaped piece back into place. Don't wet the tiny wedge as well—you don't want it to stick to your fingers or tweezers as you replace it. **NOTE** *As with all tasks in clay, there is a beautiful moment to do any job, and if you miss it, the clay fights you. If you hit it, the job is easy. For assembling chain with ease, your magical moment is just as the clay slips from hard leather-hard into bone-dry, or when the links are completely bone-*

TIP | WHY NOT USE SLIP TO GLUE MY WEDGES BACK IN PLACE?

You might be tempted to use slip instead of water to rejoin the cut rings, but I'd encourage you not to. Slip tends to work more as a glue than as a joining agent, and that makes a weaker join because slip, being a slurry, has more water and less metal than the solid clay body. It also makes a mess, and, when used as a glue, requires clean up by filing, sanding, or carving later. Slip might also tend to fill in your textured areas, whereas a thin wash of water will allow you to make a seamless connection of textured surfaces.

An assembled chain, inspected, dry, and ready to fire. I did patinate the half of the rings that were fired, even though the patina will burn off in the kiln. I find that fine silver often has a "chemical memory," and the rings that had been patinated will react differently than the virgin ones when the final piece is in the liver of sulphur.

Work-hardening the finished, fired chain on an anvil, with a chasing hammer.

dry. If your clay is suitably dry, you cut your links cleanly with no chipping, and you replace the wedge well on the first shot. The links will almost suck their cut pieces back in with little to no effort from you. In that case, a quick slick across the cuts with a soft, damp paintbrush should be all you need to erase the evidence of your join. If things don't go as well, or if you're trying to do this job on clay that is still wet inside, you'll spend a lot more time cleaning up and erasing evidence of your join.

05 | Continue to join the links together, first joining sets of two links into threes, all of the threes into sevens, and the sevens into fifteens, etc. This gives the previous joins a chance to set up and dry a bit before the set is picked up and handled.

06 | Let the joined chain dry thoroughly. Inspect the cut links to see if any require touchup with a damp brush. Lay the whole chain out on a kiln shelf. Fire the chain for 2 hours at 1650° F (899° C). Don't even consider short- or underfiring your chains—you want to be able to hammer and forge your links and, if properly made, your chain will last for lifetimes. Maybe it will even be dug up two thousand years from now and shown in a museum.

07 | Remove the chain from the kiln. Don't be concerned if links have become lightly stuck together or if some have warped. You can hammer the wavy links flat quite easily, and with a good shake or a drop on the table, the tiny little sticky points will let go without any surface marring.

08 | Work-harden the chain by hammering, forging, and tumbling to taste. (Refer to the enclosed DVD for a video demonstration on hammering assembled chain. You'll see right away why it's so nice to forge finished rings for half of the chain.)

16
mechanical pendant bails

MATERIALS
16-, 14-, or 12-gauge fine silver wire
Fine silver metal clay (optional)

TOOLS
Torch
Protective tweezers or Third Hand
Kiln brick

Flat-nose pliers
Chasing hammer
Anvil
Drill or metal hole punch
Round metal file, pointed burnisher,
  or beading awl

ALTHOUGH SIMPLE bails like embedded wire U shapes are fine, you can take your work to a more professional level by experimenting with more sophisticated bails and connecting elements. One of the easiest and most functional professional attachments to make is a little mechanical bail, formed by fusing or soldering a ring through the hole pierced in a drawn bead or a rolled ball of metal clay, fired onto the end

of a piece of wire (see pages 67 and 44). Again, use fine silver wire for this. You can use sterling silver in smaller gauges of wire, but you'll lose the ability to fully fire your fine silver metal clay.

01 | Make a ball-end head pin by drawing a bead at the end of a wire (page 67) or by embedding a wire into a smoothly rolled ball of metal clay and firing it fully for 2 hours at 1650° F (899° C).

02 | Hammer the ball flat and use a drill or hole punch to pierce it. Make your hole slightly bigger than the size of the wire you'll use as the connecting ring, or, if the wire fits too snugly in the hole, ream it to size with a beading awl.

03 | Smooth the hole, if necessary, with a file, burnisher, or awl.

TIP | PIERCED U-SHAPED BAIL

For a neat riveted bail, draw a bead (page 67) on each end of a 16- or 14-gauge wire. Hammer and pierce both ends. Use round-nose pliers to bend the wire into a U shape. Use the bail for riveting to a finished piece, embedding in fresh wet clay, or firing in place with a faux rivet.

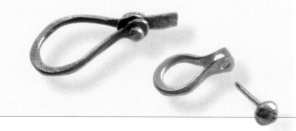

04 | Connect a fine silver jump ring through the hole. Fuse the jump ring closed (see *Fused Wire Chain*, page 69). The kiln brick makes this job simple by allowing you to place the wire, on edge, in a little channel dug in your brick so that your ring to be fused can lie flat on the block. If you can't arrange your piece so that the ring isn't touching the hole, remove the ring and ream your hole just a bit larger. You want a freely moving join.

05 | Cut the straight portion of the wire down to size in order to embed the bail into a fresh metal clay charm, link, pendant, or other item that requires a movable ring. You can cut it very short, as long as there is at least ¼" (6 mm) available to embed. Or, if it's thick enough wire to hold up on its own, such as 12-gauge, you can leave it longer.

For an embed in the front of a pendant, cut the straight wire a bit longer and use flat-nose pliers to form a 90° angle ¼" (6 mm) from one end. Push the straight wire laterally through the front of a fresh metal clay pendant pad. This type of embed works especially well for a thin piece of clay, adding structure and reinforcement. Partially embed this type of bail through the pad for a plain embed, or push it all of the way through so some of the wire sticks out the back. After firing, you can hammer the bit that shows with a riveting hammer to spread it, adding another level of reinforcement.

17
connectors

MATERIALS
16- or 14-gauge fine silver wire
Fine silver beads or rings

TOOLS
Torch
Kiln brick
Drill or hole punch
Hammer + anvil or bezel mandrel (optional)

THESE HANDY connector bars are very easy to create and can be made in any desired size. They work well as a base for other types of ornamentation, like felt or beadwork. You could use one as an arm in a riveted attachment. Or make several bars, adding heat-tolerant ornaments to each before balling the ends, and connect them together with fused fine silver rings to create an interesting chain.

01 | Cut 1" (2.5 cm) of wire.

02 | Draw a bead (page 67) on each end.

03 | Hammer each ball against the anvil to form a paddle shape.

04 | Use a drill or hole punch to pierce each paddle.

05 | If desired, attach open jump rings to each hole; fuse the rings (see *Fused wire chain*, page 69).

06 | Work-harden all fused rings with a hammer and block, anvil, or bezel mandrel.

Two styles of sculptural connector bars, formed into chains.

18
ball-end faux rivets

MATERIALS

Fired components with holes
16- or 14-gauge ball-end head pin
Fine silver metal clay
U-shaped pendant bail (optional)

TOOLS

Working surface
Roller
Rolling guides
Texture sheets or rubber stamps
Fine tissue blade

I USE THE term "faux rivet" to describe several types of connections I make with metal clay because the term "rivet" usually implies a finish that's manually applied, either by spreading wire ends with a hammer or by using mechanical force to splay or spread wire or tubing to hold other pieces together. There are several connections you can make with wire and metal clay that act as rivets, but are accomplished without mechanical force. To do this, I use ball-end rivets. Ball-ends

Using a **FAUX RIVET** to hold a U bail. The second ball end will be formed with fresh clay, and fired in place on the wire in the kiln. (See U bail tip box, below.)

are traditionally formed in the flame, but can also be accomplished by firing small rolled balls of metal clay onto the ends of wire. This technique involves trapping elements with holes on the wire, or "pinning" them to a fresh metal clay base using a previously fired or drawn ball-end head pin.

You could technically make these faux rivets by firing the ball-ends at the same time that the assembly that they connect is fired, but you run the risk of disturbing the greenware ball on the end of the wire as you construct the stack or transport your piece to the kiln. You'll have better success if you craft the head pins first, then assemble pieces that require them.

01 | For a free ball-end faux rivet, pass the head pin through one or more components and place a freshly rolled ball of clay on the other end of the wire. Allow the ball of fresh clay to dry completely.

02 | For a pinned ball-end faux rivet, prepare a fresh clay base. Pass the head pin through one or more components and embed it into the fresh clay base, forming a fixed ball-end Faux Rivet. Allow the assembly to dry completely.

03 | Fire your faux rivets fully for 2 hours at 1650° F (899° C). The trapped components will move freely between the ball and the base after firing. If they stick a bit after firing, tumble the piece to release them.

04 | Tumble the finished pieces for several hours, if possible. Hammer the top of the fixed rivet to taste to mimic a traditional finish.

TIP | U BAIL

For a different look, pin a **PIERCED U-SHAPED BAIL** (page 76) in place around a flat fresh clay pendant form, using a double ball-end faux rivet. Again, you'll have best success if you use a prepared ball-end head pin for this job so that you only have to protect one fresh clay ball embed. Allow the assembly to dry completely, and fire for 2 hours at 1600°F (899°C). After firing, the rivet and the bail should move freely. If they stick slightly out of the kiln, tumble to free them.

19
hammered rivets

COLD-JOINED RIVETS allow you to permanently connect two or more pieces of metal, through pierced or drilled holes, with a wire. This type of cold connection can be done with an embedded or soldered post or tube, which you flatten or flare at the ends to hold a collection of objects with holes together. You can also make a free rivet, a simple piece of wire with both ends flattened or flared. Rivets can be hammered down as tightly as you choose, to allow or not allow the items in the stack to spin. I generally choose movement for my pieces because things that move are more fun to wear, make people happy, and generate interest in the work.

MATERIALS
Fired metal clay pieces with holes
Base with a fixed rivet post

TOOLS
Riveting or ball-end hammer
Flush cutters
Anvil with smooth horn or metal
    ring mandrel (or both)

Fixed Rivet

01 | Finish and patina the base piece. Pull and twist the rivet post to harden it (see *Simple Rivet Posts*, page 50).

02 | Stack the metal pieces with holes on the post, arranging them so there's no empty space. Make sure the hole of the top bead cap fits the wire snugly. It's best if everything in your stack fits neatly around the wire so that the post is fully supported, but a rivet can be done if at least the top layer is snug. If everything is floppy, you simply can't do a rivet.

If you need to fill the holes of any of the stacked items, consider using spacers like tiny coils of wire, short cuts of metal tube, a stack of tiny metal rings, or large seed beads. If the top item in the stack has a filled hole, top the filled hole with a solid disk that covers the spacers to give you a solid platform on which to do your rivet.

03 | Trim the wire, leaving less than 1 mm sticking up from the stack. This part is crucial: you'll be hammering this wire end,

A nice **FIRED RIVET RING POST RING** made with two bead caps and a spinny disk.

The first cut of a rivet post should be a bit high, so that you can properly evaluate your final trim. I had a snug fit on this wire, but a deep dimple to my glass bead, so I ended up using almost all of this wire to spread into a head large enough to fill the glass dimple.

A shorter rivet wire being tapped with the chisel point of the riveting hammer to spread the top of the wire enough to trap the bead and the fine silver rivet angel but still allow the bead to spin.

so you only want to leave enough to easily spread into a head size that will comfortably cover the hole. If you leave too much, it will want to bend instead of spread. If you leave too little, it won't be enough to spread out and cover the hole. Each rivet requires a judgment call about how much to trim, and your decision will be based on how tightly the items in your stack fit the wire and the gauge of the wire. If your holes fit snugly and your fine silver wire is nice and thick (like 12-gauge), you can leave as much as $1/32$" (1 mm) sticking up to give yourself a sturdy spread head. I usually try to come as close to that ideal as possible when planning riveted stacks in fine silver.

04 | Support the base of the rivet post firmly on the horn of the anvil or metal ring mandrel. Hold the piece so the rivet post is completely vertical. Use the chisel point of the hammer to gently tap the top of the post. Turn the hammer or the piece, as necessary, to make sure wire spreads evenly. Keep the rivet post perfectly straight and go slowly. Many small taps are more effective than hard blows.

TIP | RIVET ANGELS

I often use my scrap fresh clay to cut out rivet angels: tiny flat spacers with very small pilot holes in the center. They help rivets happen easily by filling in larger holes or hugging wire more tightly than the underpinnings can.

Free Rivet

MATERIALS

Fired metal clay pieces with holes
14-, 12-, or 10-gauge fine silver wire

TOOLS

Torch
Third Hand
Tweezers

Kiln brick
Riveting or ball-end hammer
Flush cutters
Anvil with smooth horn or metal ring
    mandrel (or both)
Fine-grain sandpaper or metal file
Tumbler + mixed stainless steel shot

01 | Use the torch to draw a bead (page 67) on one end of the wire.

02 | Place the balled end of the wire on top of the small hole in the anvil or, if the anvil hole is too big, a drilled or punched hole in a coin over the anvil hole (see photos at right).

03 | Use the hammer to tap the ball to flatten it a bit. This flat section will allow you to properly support the base of the rivet while you flatten the top. Remove wire.

04 | Slide the items to be riveted onto the wire. Support the base, holding the assembly so the wire is straight up and down.

05 | Trim the wire, leaving $1/32$" (1 mm) or less sticking up from the stack. As with the fixed rivet (page 80), be sure to leave enough wire to, once hammered, spread easily into a head size that will comfortably cover the hole, but not so much that the job of spreading it becomes too difficult to accomplish.

06 | Use the chisel point of the hammer to gently tap the top of the post. Turn the hammer or the piece, as necessary, to make sure wire spreads evenly.

07 | Sand, file, or tumble the pieces to smooth the edges of the rivet heads.

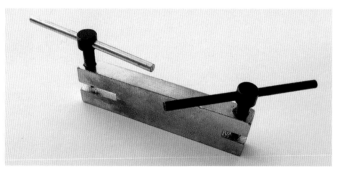

A handy two-hole punch.

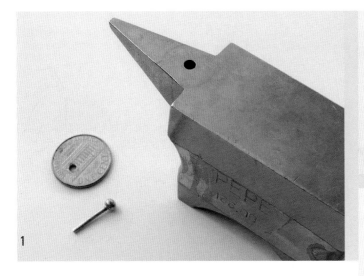

MAKING FREE RIVETS. 1. A penny, with a 16-gauge hole punched in it, to set on top of the hole in my anvil, and a 16-gauge ball-end head pin. **2.** The ball-end head pin, seated in the hole in the penny, and extending down through the hole in the anvil, ready for flattening. **3.** The flattened ball end, ready to form the base of a rivet. **4.** A circle box with a hole in the back, waiting for a free rivet to hold a bead in place in the center of the box.

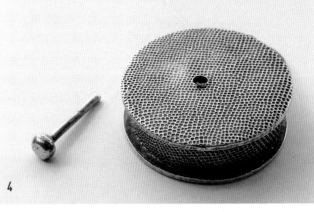

projects

What follows is a sampling of projects meant to build your metal-clay and fine-silver skills. Each of the projects featured will suggest the best path for making sure your piece is made professionally and that you assemble and fully fire each of your structural components for best results.

For these projects, you'll use the skills, components, and elements described in the book, from ball-end head pins ornamenting a *Knobby Chain* or *Stacked Rings*, to sculptural metal clay ends on wire, as in the *Sea Prong Necklace*. You'll rivet beads onto inset rivet posts in the *Rivet Post Ring*, make a free rivet with a ball-end head pin in the *Returning Ring*, and practice covering a wire armature with fresh clay in *Bird on a Branch*. The *Owl Peeking Pendant* and *Skyscraper Ring* will test your box-building skills, and the *Amphora Pendant* could be just the perfect setting for a long focal bead already in your collection.

stacked rings

These textural rings are easy to make, yet visually powerful. Wear them on your fingers or incorporate them into other pieces, either as connecting links or focals. You can easily add textural details or mechanical parts to these rings by using appliqué techniques or embedding short decorative head pins into the fresh, wet clay.

FINISHED SIZE

¼" x 1" to 1¼"
(6 x 25 to 32 mm)

MATERIALS

8–12 g fine silver metal clay

Several fine silver 6mm ball-end head pins (optional)

TOOLS

Working surface

Roller

Rolling guides

1⅜6" (30 mm) circle cutter

1" (25 mm) circle cutter

Soft paintbrush and water

Vermiculite + firing dish (optional)

Kiln posts (optional)

Kiln

Brass brush

Hammer

Anvil

Tumbler

Liver of sulfur

stacked rings

PROJECT NOTES

I pushed short-trimmed ball-end head pins into my rings so they'd match my **KNOBBY CHAIN** (page 91). These rings look lovely either with texture or plain. Once you get the hang of the stacking overlaps, they're easy to make in a variety of sizes.

TECHNIQUES + ELEMENTS

Circles + rings (page 36)
Ball-end faux rivets (page 78)

01 | Roll fresh clay 6 to 8 cards thick. **NOTE** *I don't usually texture the rolled sheets for stacking rings, as any texture will make it difficult to get a clean bond later.*

02 | Cut 3 or 4 ring shapes. For a very comfortable size 7–7½ ring, use the 1³⁄₁₆" (30 mm) cutter for the outside diameter and the 1" (25 mm) cutter for the inside diameter.

03 | If desired, embed 1 or more ball-end head pins into the edge of one or all of the rings.

04 | Let the rings become hard leather-hard or bone-dry.

05 | Use the paintbrush to apply a wash of water on each side of the rings that will be joined, keeping in mind that the embeds should be staggered and that any texture will make it difficult to get a clean bond on the areas to be joined. Firmly squidge each ring to its partner until you feel them grab. Let each attachment set up a bit before you add more.

Two **STACKED RINGS**, with embedded **BALL-END HEAD PINS**, squidged together and ready to fire. I am hanging the ring to the right off of the end of the kiln post to accommodate the second **BALL-END HEAD PIN** embedded into the bottom layer of the ring and just visible in between the posts.

06 | Let the rings dry thoroughly, then fully fire. To fire rings with embeds on both the top and bottom, set them on kiln posts and hang the embeds off the edge, or set the rings in a dish of vermiculite.

07 | Work-harden the finished rings by lightly hammering or tumbling. Hammer the embeds to flatten them like rivets, if you like. **NOTE** *If your rings come apart when you hammer them, you need to work on your squidging technique.*

08 | Brush, tumble, and patina the rings as desired.

knobby chain

When I first learned to make metal clay chain, it was so exciting: deciding where to cut the link; settling on the keystone wedge shape, choosing the perfect moment to cut, and being able to make chain with intricate texture. But making simple links like those in this chain has a draw, too—the simplicity of the smooth surfaces is pure design power.

FINISHED SIZE
17" x ¾"
(43.2 x 1.9 cm)

MATERIALS
75 g of fine silver metal clay
7–20 fine silver 3mm ball-end head pins
3" (7.6 cm) of fine silver 12-gauge wire

TOOLS
Work surface
Roller
Rolling guides
Texture sheets or rubber stamps
   (optional)
Various circle cutters from
   ⁵⁄₁₆"–1" (8–28 mm) wide
Jeweler's tweezers (optional)
Sharp tissue blade
Soft paintbrush + water
Kiln
Brass brush
Tumbler (optional)
Liver of sulfur (optional)
Large round-nose pliers
   or small Wrap + Tap tool
Chasing hammer
Metal ring mandrel
Anvil

knobby chain

PROJECT NOTES

This project is a great way to show off your forging prowess. When your first rings come out of the kiln, give your attention to each one. Would you like your links to be absolutely flat? Use a chasing hammer to lightly tap both sides on an anvil. Would you like them to be totally round? Put them on a mandrel and hammer gently around the edge, spinning the link until it's rounded to your taste. Do you enjoy hammer texture or deep forging? Lay it on.

TECHNIQUES + ELEMENTS

Circles + rings (page 36)
Ball-end faux rivets (page 78)
Metal clay chain (page 73)

01 | Roll a sheet of metal clay 8 cards thick and texture if desired.

02 | Use the circle cutters to cut out 34 to 40 rings. They can all be the same size or different. For this piece, I used smaller rings to connect the larger, but your choice of ring sizes is just that—a choice—and will dramatically affect the look and wear of your finished piece. Experiment!

03 | Use the tweezers to embed a previously fired (or drawn) fine silver ball-end head pin into the side of one of the larger rings. Repeat to add the remaining head pins anywhere on the larger rings you like. Be sure that you've trimmed the head pins close enough so that the ends of the wire don't protrude through the other side of the ring, or, if you choose to totally pierce the rings during embedding, you can trim the protruding wire flush after firing with sharp flush cutters, leaving an interesting mark on the inside of each ring. Don't set many embeds in the smaller rings, as you'll need to cut them to assemble the chain.

04 | Let the rings dry. Fully fire the large rings and set the unfired smaller rings aside.

05 | Forge the fired rings to your liking and set aside. Keep in mind that these rings will alternate with the unfired rings, so this is a good time to plan for an alternating pattern if you'd like. If so, focus on making this set of rings visually distinct from the second set. **NOTE** *This step is not for work-hardening the rings, only for appearance. The second firing will render them all dead soft again.*

Plain and **KNOBBY RINGS**, forged and textured and ready to build into chain, by being joined with cut dry clay links. (See **METAL CLAY CHAIN**, page 73.)

Forging the embedded **BALL-END HEAD PINS** after firing to form thick, flat, paddles. Much larger beads can be formed with clay balls than can be drawn with fire.

06 | Use a sharp, clean tissue blade to cut small wedge-shaped pieces out of each bone-dry ring. Use the paintbrush and a bit of water on the receiving end of the links to rejoin the rings around two fired rings, creating a short chain (page 73). If your cuts are clean, and you have the cut wedge in right-side up, the bone-dry links will almost suck their cut

pieces back in, making your job simple. Connect the rings into groups of three, let them set up, then connect the threes into sevens, and the sevens into fifteens. Add links as necessary for fit. Let the chain dry completely. Inspect it for evidence of your cuts. If things went well cutting and replacing your wedges, your cuts should be almost invisible. If you can see any marks, gaps, or lines, clean them up with a dampened paintbrush or a bit of lightly dampened fine sandpaper. Try to avoid dry-sanding metal clay, as it creates talc-fine metal dust, which can get into your pores and lungs.

07 | Fully fire the chain for 2 hours at 1650° F (899° C). Hammer the links to work-harden them, both flat on an anvil and around a steel ring mandrel. Brush, tumble, and patina to taste.

08 | Use the round-nose pliers or the Wrap and Tap tool to bend the 12-gauge wire into an S-clasp. Work-harden the clasp and texture as desired. Attach the clasp to one end of the chain.

rivet post ring

One of the easiest and most useful projects I make with embedded rivet posts is this simple and elegant ring. Such rings are great for fingers, for use as pendant bails, or for more whimsical designs, such as rings with moveable and spinning components.

FINISHED SIZE
Size 6 to 8 ring with
⁵⁄₁₆" x ⁷⁄₁₆" (7 x 11 mm) ring top

MATERIALS
4–6 g fine silver metal clay
½" (1.3 cm) of fine silver
  14- or 12-gauge wire
1 lampworked 7x11mm bead
  or other bead or ornament

TOOLS
Working surface
Roller
Rolling guides
Texture sheets or rubber stamps
  (optional)
1³⁄₁₆" (30 mm) circle cutter
1" (25 mm) circle cutter
Flush cutters
Kiln
Brass brush
Flat-nose pliers
Hammer
Anvil
Metal ring mandrel or anvil
  with smooth horn (or both)
Tumbler (optional)
Liver of sulfur (optional)

Lampworked bead by Sarah Moran

rivet post ring

PROJECT NOTES

I've listed specific cutter measurements, but you may need different sizes depending on your desired ring size. With these cutters, the finished ring will fit a size 6 to 8 after firing and basic work-hardening. Keep in mind that you can always size a ring up with a hammer and ring mandrel (or anvil horn), but you can't make it smaller, so don't cut the inside diameter more than 5% larger than your final desired size. You want to allow not only for shrinkage, but also to give you room to work-harden your ring in on a mandrel without exceeding your finished size. I also use fine silver wire in all of my metal clay work; this is because I like to be able to fully fire my metal clay at 1650° F (899° C), but admittedly, if you use sterling wire, you can make the choice to sacrifice some of the density of the fine silver band to get harder wire in a smaller gauge.

Choose your post thickness based on both the destiny of your piece and the hole size of your ornaments. Make sure that the hole fits snugly on either 14- or 12-gauge fine silver wire without rattling around. If it doesn't, then you'll need to build spacers or shims, coil wire, or cut tube to fill the gap between the bead and the post. I find that 16-gauge wire is generally too small to choose for a rivet post in fine silver; it may technically work, but there won't be enough material to spread up top to guarantee a long-wearing rivet. If you're making ornaments for earrings, a 16-gauge rivet in fine silver may be fine, but for structurally sound pieces, such as rings, that need to stand up to heavy wear, don't use fine silver embed posts in gauges smaller than 14.

TECHNIQUES + ELEMENTS

Circles + rings (page 36)
Simple rivet posts (page 50)
Hammered rivets (page 80)

01 | Roll and, if desired, texture a sheet of clay 8 to 10 cards thick. Use the 1³/₁₆" (30 mm) circle cutter to cut the ring's outside diameter and the 1" (25 mm) cutter to cut the ring's inside diameter.

02 | Smooth the cuts with your fingers to avoid unnecessary filing or sanding later.

03 | Smoothly embed the wire into the edge of the ring in one motion. Push this rivet post all the way through the ring body until it's just about to emerge from the inside curve. This may create a soft bump on the inside of the ring, but it feels nice when worn. If the wire ends up protruding more than you like, you can trim it with sharp flush cutters after the ring is fired. It may also smooth out to your satisfaction during the riveting process; the bump will be against the mandrel or anvil horn as you are hammering the top of the wire. Don't handle the embed or the ring at all until it's completely dry.

04 | After the ring is bone-dry, fully fire flat on a kiln shelf. The rivet post will be dead soft when it comes out of the kiln, so it should be work-hardened. The

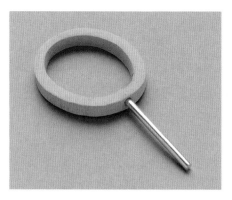

A **RIVET POST RING** base, bone-dry and ready to fire. Note the clean, tight wire embed.

best way to work-harden the post is, unbelievably, to hold the piece in your hand and grab the end of the wire with flat-nose pliers. Pull hard from both directions and twist the wire a quarter to a full turn. This straightens and hardens the post. It's scary the first time and lots of fun every time after that, unless you don't place your embeds well enough and they pop out. If that happens, just drill out the hole and make a free rivet.

05 | Finish the ring blank to taste before placing your ornament. Hammer the ring body from all directions, including on a ring mandrel or anvil horn. This will, of course, size up your ring, so be aware of the progress you're making toward your finished size. Complete all sizing and finishing, brushing, patinating, and tumbling before you add any ornaments to the rivet post.

06 | Place the ornaments on the post and either bend, squeeze, or rivet the wire end so the elements are trapped on the wire. You may choose to tamp the ornaments down tightly or leave room for them to spin. A useful technique for completing a clean rivet, yet still allowing spin in the finished piece, is to place thin paper or plastic spacers in the rivet stack, complete the rivet, and then either pull, burn, or soak out the spacers.

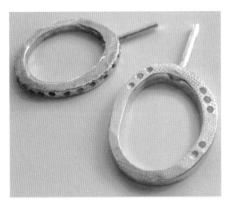

Finished, fired **RIVET POST RINGS**, waiting for their beads or spinners.

sea prong necklace

This lively neckpiece seems different in every light and on every neck. It dances. The technique involved in creating it is simple and gives you great flexibility as a designer; every choice you make when sculpting your head pins will dramatically affect the look of the finished piece.

FINISHED SIZE
20¼" (51.4 cm)

MATERIALS
25–50 g of fine silver metal clay
2–3' (61–91.5 cm) of fine silver
  14- or 12-gauge wire
3 fine silver 1" (2.5 cm) ball-end head pins
4" (10.2 cm) of fine silver 18- or 16-gauge
  wire (optional, for prong settings)
2 peridot 5x10mm faceted oval stones
3 fine silver 10mm jump rings
Solder (optional)
1 fine silver 20x34mm
  sculptural S-clasp

TOOLS
Working surface
Roller
Rolling guides
Texture sheet (optional)
Various circle cutters, ⁵⁄₁₆"–1" (8–25 mm)
  wide
Kiln
Brass brush
Hammer
Anvil
Wire cutters
Metal hole punch or drill with tiny bit
Round metal needle file or beading awl
Large round-nose pliers, dowel,
  mandrel, or Wrap + Tap tool
Flat-nose pliers
Torch (optional)
Kiln brick (optional)
Liver of sulfur
Tumbler
Burnisher (optional)

sea prong necklace

PROJECT NOTES

I made the **SEA PRONG** connections with fine silver metal clay rings, but since the double-ended head pins are simply wrapped around each ring to connect the elements, you can use any type (or mix of types) of connecting ring that pleases you. A mix of metal clay and fused fine silver rings always looks nice. Experiment, because each choice you make will change the look of your piece.

Learning to sculpt the head pin ends smoothly around the fine silver wire is something that takes practice; don't be discouraged if you overwork your first efforts and your **SEA PRONG** tips are a little rough. Your fingers will learn to move rapidly to form your desired shapes so that you're handling the clay as little as possible. Also, as with all sculptural jobs in metal clay, the fresher your clay is, the easier it will be to get what you want.

I chose to set a couple of pieces of peridot at the bottom of my focal prongs—you can do this, too; any stone will work, because the gems are not being fired with the silver.

TECHNIQUES + ELEMENTS

Head pins (page 44)
Prongs (page 65)
Sculptural S-clasp (page 46)
Circles + rings (page 36)
Metal clay chain (page 73)
Mechanical pendant bail (page 76)
Fused wire chain (page 69)

01 | LARGE RINGS AND CHAINS.

Roll the clay out, texturing if desired, to end up with a thickness of 4–6 cards. Use the various circle cutters to cut 13 or more thin-walled rings, each between ⁷/₁₆" (18 mm) and 1" (25 mm) in diameter. Smooth the cuts with your fingers and pull some into oval shapes if desired. Let these large rings become hard leather-hard to bone-dry. Use 4 of the rings to form 1 short metal clay chain, 2 of the rings to form another. Set aside for firing.

2 | SMALL RINGS.

Roll the clay out, texturing if desired, to end up with a thickness of 3–4 cards. Use the various circle cutters to cut 6 or more rings, each about ³/₈" (1 cm) in diameter. Smooth the cuts with your fingers. Let these small rings dry completely, and set aside.

03 | SEA PRONGS.

Cut 2" (5.1 cm) of 14- or 12-gauge wire. Slide 1 small bone-dry clay ring (from Step 2) onto the wire. Place a smoothly rolled ball of fresh metal clay on each end, capturing the bone-dry ring on the wire. Sculpt and form the balls into pleasing shapes that flow into the wire, with the bulk of the clay at each wire end and the ring loose on the wire. Texture as desired. Set aside.

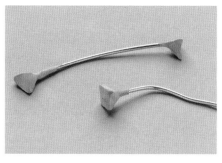

Several **SEA PRONG** elements ready for firing.

Repeat this entire step to make 8 double-ended sculptural head pins between 2 and 3" (5.1 and 7.6 cm) long, some with rings, some without. Let them dry completely and set aside for firing.

04 | SEA PRONG SETTINGS.

Cut 2"–3" (5.1–7.6 cm) of 14- or 12-gauge wire. Place a smoothly rolled ball of fresh metal clay on one end. Sculpt and form the ball into a pleasing shape with one flat side large enough to accommodate your gemstone, allowing a bit of extra space in your setting for shrinkage. Texture and embellish as desired. Cut three to five ³/₁₆" (5 mm) pieces of 18- or 16-gauge wire for your setting. The size and length of the pieces will depend on the size of your necklace and what cut of gem or stone you'll be setting. (To set my peridot oval, I cut four ¹/₂" [1.3 cm] pieces

Three **SEA PRONG CHARMS**, hammered and pierced, with fine silver rings fused into each. These were gathered onto one larger fused fine silver ring to include in the finished **SEA PRONG NECKLACE** (see photo at right.)

of 18-gauge fine silver wire and trimmed them further to fit the stone after firing.) Embed the pieces of cut wire into the base of the clay to make a prong setting for the tiny gem. **NOTE** *The gemstones will be added after firing. Repeat to make at least one more sea prong setting and let dry fully. Set aside for firing.*

05 | SEA PRONG CHARMS. Place a smoothly rolled ball of fresh metal clay at the straight end of one ball-end head pin. Sculpt and form the ball into a pleasing shape; texture as desired. Place a small ¹/₁₆"–¹/₈" (2–3 mm) smoothly rolled ball of fresh clay on the other end, and leave it round. (This ball will be hammered flat and pierced after firing.) Let the charm dry fully and set aside for firing. Repeat this entire step with the remaining 2 head pins, to make three sea prong charms of varying length.

06 | Fire all of the sea prongs, settings, and charms fully. Brush and tumble to taste.

07 | Hammer the ball-ends of each of the 3 sea prong charms made in Step 5 flat against the anvil. Use a hole punch or drill to pierce the flattened area of each head pin and clean the holes with a file or beading awl. Set aside.

08 | Use the sea prongs from Step 3 to connect the loose rings and chains. Do so by using large round-nose pliers, dowels, mandrels, or a Wrap and Tap tool to bend the head pins into interesting shapes, connecting the rings into a

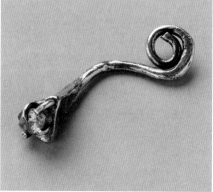

An alluring **SEA PRONG** setting, with a lovely curled Fern Frond end.

VARIATIONS

This design can be used in a variety of ways. A double **SEA PRONG** makes a beautiful ring, especially when formed on 12-gauge fine silver wire and curved into an elegant shape. A shortened version of the necklace makes a delightful bracelet, and a single **SEA PRONG** works well as a pendant.

A set of **SEA PRONG CHARMS** makes a lovely stand-alone pendant.

10 | Patina and tumble the necklace to your satisfaction. Set the gemstones into the sea prong settings. Tumble again, if possible, to smooth and harden the settings. If your stones don't like the tumbler, use a burnisher to harden the prongs.

11 | Make any adjustments to the piece that you like. You may have to play with the curves and angles of your attachments to make sure that the necklace lies smoothly around your neck, or you may choose to add, subtract, or rearrange elements to make the piece your own.

kinetic chain. Use 1 jump ring to attach each of the three pierced, ball-end sea prongs to one of the rings on the chain. If desired, fuse or solder the jump rings.

09 | Form a wire spiral at the end of one of the sea prongsettings. Slide the spiral onto the second sea prong setting. Bend the second sea prong setting into an interesting shape and connect it to one end of the chain formed in Step 8. Use a hammer and anvil to work-harden the wire. Add the S-clasp to the other end of the chain.

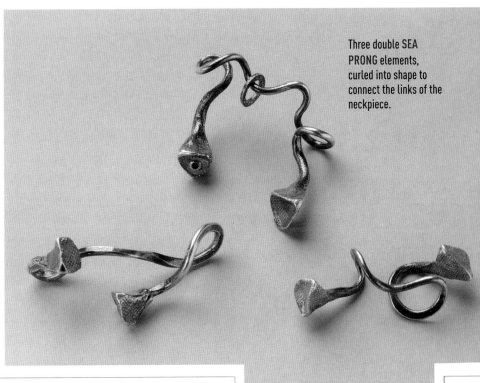

Three double SEA PRONG elements, curled into shape to connect the links of the neckpiece.

circlet
of flowers
necklace

Take a beautiful handful of
fine silver flowers and join them
together into an elegant and
fanciful chain. The shape of these
flowers was inspired by the deep
cup and rounded petal tip of the
Saguaro cactus, a bloom that is
as ephemeral as it is surprising;
who would expect these tall desert
warriors to have such tender, deep
red blooms?

FINISHED SIZE
17" (43.2 cm)

MATERIALS

50–75 g fine silver metal clay

12 fine silver 13x18mm 14-gauge
     oval jump rings + 1 fine silver 16mm
     14-gauge round jump ring or 2'
     (61 cm) of 14-gauge fine silver wire

3" (7.6 cm) of 12-gauge fine silver wire

TOOLS

Working surface

Roller

Rolling guides

Texture sheets or rubber stamps

Sharp tissue blade, craft knife,
     or razor blade

Sharp 1⁵⁄₁₆" (4 cm) five-petal
     flower-shaped cookie cutter

Sharp 1³⁄₁₆" (3 cm) four-petal
     flower-shaped cookie cutter

Curved drying base (marbles, small
     wooden balls, Styrofoam balls, round
     Christmas bulbs, or tiny eggs)

Soft paintbrush and water

Dapping block

¹¹⁄₁₆" (17 mm) + ⁷⁄₈" (22 mm) circle
     cutters

Cocktail straw

Round-end burnisher or beading awl

Chasing hammer

Anvil

Vermiculite + firing dish (optional)

Kiln

Brass brush

Liver of sulfur

Tumbler

Torch

Kiln brick

Flat-nose pliers

circlet of flowers necklace

PROJECT NOTES

Sturdy jump rings could easily be substituted for fused or soldered rings; you may wish to do this if you are not expert at fusing or soldering. This is an advanced flame-joining job because the attachments are bulky and it's difficult to isolate the joint of a jump ring flat on the block with two large flowers on each side of it. I like a challenge, and I like fused rings, so I closed my rings with fire.

TECHNIQUES + ELEMENTS

Sculptural S-clasp (page 46)
Fused wire chain (page 69)
Circles + rings (page 36)

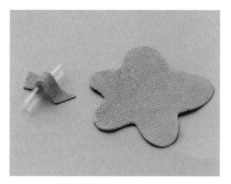

Above: A freshly cut flower shape and a strap bail band, drying over a drinking straw. *Top right:* A cut flower drying over a rounded form (I used a half-tablespoon measure). *Bottom right:* A cut flat flower link, waiting to be fired and dapped, and a completed flower with a strap band bail attached, being allowed to dry fully on the form before firing.

01 | Roll the clay 4 cards thick. Texture the top of the clay, ending up with a finished roll about 3 cards thick. Use the five-petal cookie cutter to cut 12 to 16 flower shapes. Place each flower over a curved drying base, textured side up, and let them become hard leather-hard to bone-dry.

02 | Roll fresh clay 1–2 cards thick. Use the blade to cut a ¼" × ¾" (6 × 19 mm) rectangular strip to serve as a strap bail. Lay the strap bail over a drinking straw so it curves in the middle and let it become hard leather-hard to bone-dry. Repeat to make as many strap bails as you have large flowers. Thinner strap bails are easier to use, as they are more flexible and will conform more readily to the shape of the flowers.

03 | When both the flowers and the bails are hard leather-hard to bone-dry, use the paintbrush and a small bit of water to wet the ends of 1 strap bail and the spots on the flower to which it will attach. Squidge the bail to the back of a five-petal flower. Repeat to add bails to each five-petal flower. If desired, add bone-dry ornaments such as flat-bottomed dry balls to the inside of one or more flowers. Let the flowers dry completely and set aside for firing. You'll fire them sitting on a kiln shelf, or, if you have complex curves, nested in vermiculite. **NOTE** *As long as the flowers are completely bone-dry when fired, they should not slump on the shelf.*

04 | Roll and texture one or both sides of fresh clay, ending up with a finished slab about 3 cards thick. Use the four-petal cookie cutter to cut 11 to 15 flower shapes. Use the cocktail straw to cut holes in the tips of opposite petals on each flower, but not too close to the edges. I usually leave at least $^1/_{32}$" (1 mm) between a hole and an edge. Use the burnisher or beading awl to gently clean the holes from the back to avoid having to file them later. Let them dry flat and set aside for firing. **NOTE** *I chose to fire these spacers flat and dap them after they were fired because they are structural links and I like the compressive sturdiness of making them that way, but if you prefer,*

dry the flowers over curved forms and fire them nestled in vermiculite.

05 | Roll and texture both sides of fresh clay to a finished thickness of 4 cards. Use the circle cutters to form a ring. Smooth the cuts with your fingers. Let thoroughly dry and set aside for firing.

06 | Use the 12-gauge wire and some fresh clay to create a 22×34mm sculptural S-clasp. Let completely dry and set aside for firing.

07 | Fully fire your components at 1650° F (899° C) for two hours. After firing, clean the components by tumbling for 15 minutes to two hours depending on your taste for patina and shine. **NOTE** *Heavily burnished or tumbled pieces do not take patina as readily or as deeply as more porous surfaces, and you will probably want to patina them later.*

08 | Place a four-petal flower link in a dapping block divot and use the hammer and dapping peg to shape it into a nice curve; repeat with all the four-petal flower links. Clean the holes, if necessary, with a bead awl or pointed burnisher.

A pretty **SCULPTURAL S-HOOK** closes the **CIRCLET OF FLOWERS**.

09 | Use the jump rings to connect the large and small flowers into a pleasing chain, adding 1 large flower and the metal clay ring to one end link and the clasp to the other end link. If desired, fuse or solder the connecting rings and stretch them into ovals using your round-nose pliers from the inside of the ring. Use a hammer and anvil to work-harden the fused rings and clasp. Tumble, brush, and patina the finished piece as desired.

returning ring

This ring was made for Marcia DeCoster, inspired when she bought two beautiful pewter birds from my friends at Green Girl Studios. She showed me the birds and said, "What do you think?" I said, "I think I need to make a ring for you!" The happenstance conversation turned into a trade: she made a fantastic beadworked tower for me and I made this fanciful ring for her.

FINISHED SIZE
ring top 1¼" x 1⅛" x 1"
(3.2 x 2.9 x 2.5 cm)

MATERIALS
10–15 g of fine silver clay
8" (20.3 cm) of fine silver 12-gauge wire
8" (20.3 cm) of 14-gauge fine silver wire
1 pewter 8x22mm sitting bird bead
1 pewter 20mm flying bird bead
1 fine silver ½" (1.3 cm) head pin with 5mm ball end.

TOOLS
Flush cutters
Torch
Protective tweezers or Third Hand
Kiln brick
Chasing hammer
Anvil
Drill or hole punch
Metal file or beading awl
Metal ring mandrel or Wrap + Tap tool
Round-nose pliers
Flat- or chain-nose pliers
Tumbler
Working surface
Roller
Rolling guides
Texture sheets or rubber stamps
Sharp tissue blade
¼" (6 mm) circle cutters or drinking straw
Cocktail straw
Soft paintbrush + water
Vermiculite + fire-proof dish
Brass brush
Liver of sulfur

returning ring

PROJECT NOTES

A ring like this can be exciting and challenging to wear. I think of it as an event piece, or as a deliberate gift to the people you encounter in the world. I left room under the rivets so that the wearer can change the attitude of each bird. Slight adjustments, as you can see from these photos, tell vastly different stories. My favorite view is of the male, returning to the nest, to spell the female or bring her a piece of food.

TECHNIQUES + ELEMENTS

Drawing a bead (page 67)
Simple rivet posts (page 50)
Wire ring bands (page 58)
Circles + rings (page 36)
Appliqué (page 24)
Bead caps (page 42)
Hammered rivets (page 80)
Free rivet (page 82)

01 | Cut ⅝" (1.6 cm) of 12-gauge wire to use as a rivet post. Set aside.

02 | Cut 1¼" (3.2 cm) of 12-gauge wire. Use a torch to draw a bead at one end. Hammer the resultant ball flat and punch or drill a hole through it. I made my hole large enough to accept a piece of 14-gauge wire, which is what I used to attach my flying bird bead. Use round- or flat-nose pliers to bend the pierced end of the post into a J shape with the hook ½" (1.3 cm) from the ball end. Set aside.

03 | Use 14-gauge wire and either a ring mandrel or Wrap and Tap tool to form 2 matching wire ring bands. Set aside.

04 | Use fresh clay to form an ¹¹⁄₁₆" (18 mm) bead cap. Fully fire, dap, and finish as required. Set aside.

05 | Roll and texture fresh metal clay 4 to 6 cards thick. Or, if you're just learning, do yourself a favor and roll 6 cards thick to embed ring shanks and rivet posts. Embeds are easier in thicker pads. Rings become heavier, though, so as you become proficient, you may choose to use thinner pads for less weight and materials cost.

06 | Use the tissue blade to cut one 1⁵⁄₃₂" × 1¾" (29 × 45 mm) diamond-shaped pad and one ¹⁵⁄₁₆" x 1¼" (23 × 32 mm) diamond-shaped pad. Use the straws to cut two ¼" (6 mm) rings.

07 | Embed the 2 ring bands into the back of the large diamond fairly close together. You can place them directly next to each other, or as much as ¼" (6 mm) apart. Don't place them farther apart than that unless you're using sterling wire and underfiring or using 12-gauge fine silver wire. You don't want your shanks to bend apart. Don't handle the embedded shanks or the diamond *at all* until the assembly is bone-dry. This is vitally important to the success of the embeds. You might wish to move your diamonds to a kiln shelf for easy drying, and then place your embeds into the clay directly on the shelf.

08 | Appliqué the two fresh-clay ¼" (6 mm) circles to the top of the small diamond, one at each long point. The size and shape of these appliqués is not important; they are simply there to help support the posts. While the clay is still fresh and pliable, move quickly to embed the two rivet posts into the pad as shown, through center of the rings. Again, you should probably do this on your drying shelf. Don't handle the assembly until it's bone-dry.

09 | Let both pads become hard leather-hard or bone-dry. Use a bit of water on the joining side of each diamond to firmly squidge them together, flat sides facing. Be careful not to bump or damage the embeds. Let the assembly dry completely, and fire it fully, nestled gently in a dish of vermiculite. Work-harden, brush, tumble, and patina the finished ring base. Set aside.

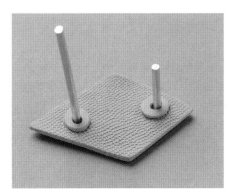

The two rivet posts, embedded into the fresh pad of clay. The taller post will be balled, hammered, pierced, and bent after the ring is fired.

10 | Slide the finished cap and 1 bird bead onto the straight wire. Trim the wire and rivet it.

11 | Use the head pin to form a free rivet, attaching the flying bird bead to the bent wire post. As you work, support the bottom of the free rivet on the tip of the flat horn of the anvil.

Riveting the sitting bird and her bead cap nest onto the shorter rivet post.

owl peeking pendant

Circle boxes tend to take on the personality of what fills them; in this case it's a small crabby owl bead. Sizing your box to match your bead may be a matter of trial and error, so you can't go wrong making a few of these in slightly different sizes and filling each one differently. The possibilities are endless.

FINISHED SIZE
pendant 1⅛"x ½"
(2.9 x 1.3 cm)

MATERIALS
25–50 g of fine silver clay
2" (5.1 cm) fine silver 12-gauge head pin with 5mm ball-end head pin
1 20mm vertical-hole lampworked owl bead
1 fired metal clay 12mm ring
28" (71.1 cm) of commercial necklace chain
1 fine or sterling silver 8mm jump ring

TOOLS
Working surface
Roller
Rolling guides
Texture sheets or rubber stamps
Sharp tissue blade
Soft paintbrush + water
1⅜" (35 mm) circle cutter
1" (25 mm) circle cutter
⁵⁄₁₆" (8 mm) circle cutter
³⁄₁₆" (5 mm) circle cutter (or drinking straw)
Vermiculite + firing dish (optional)
Kiln
Brass brush
Liver of sulfur (optional)
Tumbler (optional)
Large round-nose pliers
Hammer
Anvil

Lampworked bead by Karen Elmquist

owl peeking pendant

PROJECT NOTES

If you'd like a little more mystery to your piece, create a shadow-box effect by cutting out another circle or ring to frame the opening and appliquéing it to the box top before firing. You can also rivet a spinny lid to the top of the box post-firing—just be sure to add a pilot hole in the top piece, and an embed post or hole in the bottom piece for easy riveting. Experiment!

TECHNIQUES + ELEMENTS

Circles + rings (page 36)
Box-building (page 60)
Simple rivet posts (page 50)
Fused wire chain (page 69)

01 | Roll the clay 3 to 4 cards thick, texturing one side only (because it's difficult to make clean attachments in a box if the pieces you are sticking together have texture). Use the 1³⁄₁₆" (35 mm) circle cutter to cut two circles. Use the 1" (25 mm) circle cutter to cut out the centers of each circle. Smooth the cuts with your fingers to avoid having to sand or file later. Let these large rings become hard leather-hard to bone-dry; set aside.

02 | Roll fresh clay 2 to 3 cards thick. Use a sharp tissue blade to cut a ½" × 4½"(1.5 × 11.4 cm) rectangular strip to use as the side of the box. Quickly use the 5 mm circle cutter or section of a drinking straw to cut 9 evenly spaced holes along the strip before your strip begins to dry. Immediately after cutting the holes, form the strip into the round, forming a circular spacer. Let it dry on edge to become hard leather-hard to bone-dry. You can clean up the holes later; the most important thing is to get that spacer bent smoothly into a circle without cracking.

03 | If you like, once your spacer is hard leather-hard or bone-dry, add a few

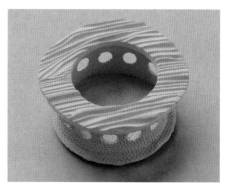

The finished greenware box, ready to fire flat on a kiln shelf.

TIP | DRYING

I use the same nifty little plastic paint cups I use to store my leftover clay to hold the shape of my circular spacers and finger rings while they dry. They are perfectly sized to allow the clay to dry around the inside of the cup. This is preferable to letting circular forms dry around the outside of a form, as the clay shrinks while it dries and will either stick to or pull away from a form that fills its interior too tightly.

appliqué details. Roll the clay 2 cards thick, and lightly texture on 1 side only so one side is smooth for appliqué. Use a ¼"–⁵⁄₁₆" (6–8 mm) circle cutter to cut one or more circles. Use the ³⁄₁₆" (5 mm) circle cutter or a large drinking straw to cut out the center of the circle. **NOTE** *It's easier to use drinking straws for cutting*

TIP | 3 HANGING IDEAS

Clockwise from upper left: a fused ring catches the box holes and a hanging ring; holes for head pins; and a rivet post box with a U-shaped metal clay bail inserted into the gap in the circle spacer.

holes if you trim them into 1" or 2" (2.5 or 5.1 cm) segments first. They're easier to hold onto, not as likely to bend, and it makes it easier to retrieve the cut piece from the straw. Place your appliqués onto the hard leather-hard or bone-dry box side while they are still fresh and supple. That way it's easy to form them around the curved side.

04 | Use the paintbrush and a small bit of water to squidge the edge of the circular spacer to the smooth side of one large ring, then wet and squidge the smooth side of the second large ring to the other edge of the circular spacer, forming a box. Either bring the edges of the spacer together (it will be slightly flexible) and fill the resulting seam with a tiny snake of fresh clay after your box is set, as I did in this piece and as I do for my *My First Kiss Pipe Rings* (page 62), or intentionally leave a gap to insert a dry metal clay hanging bail. Let the assembled box dry thoroughly and fully fire, either flat on a kiln shelf, or, if you have an odd shape or delicate protrusions, in a dish of vermiculite.

05 | Clean, tumble, and patina the box form to taste.

06 | Place the owl bead inside the box so the bead holes line up with holes on the sides of the box. Slide the head pin through one of these side holes, the bead, and the opposite side hole. Bend the wire end in a 90° angle at the top of the box. Use round-nose pliers to form a simple loop to secure the bead in place. Use a hammer and edge of an anvil to work-harden the loop.

07 | Open the loop and slide on the 12mm fired metal clay ring.

08 | String the chain through the 12mm ring. Use the jump ring to connect the chain ends.

I tried a variety of owls in my box before choosing one. **Bead by Karen Elmquist.**

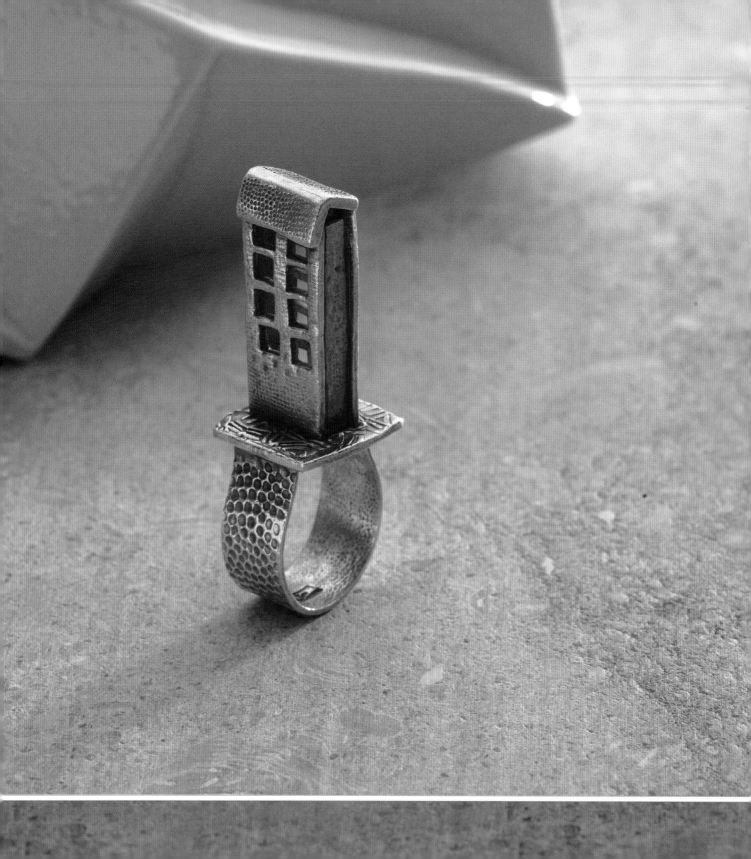

skyscraper ring

My friend had a dream about the two of us searching downtown Chicago for the perfect studio space. In it we discovered a penthouse in a ratty old space with a great view of the lake. The dream inspired me to sculpt little buildings in every sort of shape I could think up. When I showed them all to Scott, he pointed unhesitatingly to this one and said, "It was here." I named the series "Scott's Dream."

FINISHED SIZE
ring top (with roof)
1¼" x ½" x ¼"
(32 x 13 x 6 mm)

MATERIALS
25–50 g of fine silver metal clay

Fired + finished fine silver metal clay strap ring band, of a width and weight suitable to support the size of your finished building.

Paper

TOOLS
Working surface

Roller

Rolling guides

Texture sheets or rubber stamps

Sharp tissue blade

Various shape cutters such as tiny squares for windows (optional)

Soft paintbrush + water

Kiln

Hammer

Metal ring mandrel

Tumbler (optional)

Brass brush

Liver of sulfur

skyscraper ring

PROJECT NOTES

When making buildings, you should consider whether or not you're going to want doors and windows when you choose your style, size, and texture pattern. I always cut windows, both for design interest and to reduce the weight of my piece, but oddly, I never want a door. (I'm told that this is a psychological "tell" of an intensely private person.) There are many texture sheets available that simulate stone, brick, concrete, and rock; experiment with both realism and fancy in your exteriors. Roofs can be difficult to get just right; you have to think like an architect. I almost never cut my roof until my building is completely assembled. This gives me a better sense of what would fit stylistically.

TECHNIQUES + ELEMENTS

Metal clay ring bands (page 52)
Box-building (page 60)

01 | Roll and texture fresh clay 6 cards thick. Cut a ⅝"–⅞" (15–22 mm) pad of any shape to use as the ring top's base. Embed the fired, formed strap band into the pad. Try to do your embed in one smooth motion, pushing it in deeply enough to almost push through the pad. Set the assembly aside and let it dry completely. Watch it while it dries to make sure it doesn't warp. If it starts to do so, gently press the pad back down flat against the drying surface without picking up the still-wet assembly.

02 | Use the paper to cut out pattern pieces for your planned building, keep-

A finished, fired strap band ring shank bent into a lovely oval form and embedded into a fresh clay pad. The bone-dry skyscraper can be squidged onto the dry pad later.

ing in mind that the pad created in the previous step will serve as the base. Remember that this building will need to fit on your finger, so it's a good idea, if you want a wearable ring, to keep it under 2" (5.1 cm) tall and 1" (2.5 cm) in diameter. Making a paper or light cardboard model will be very helpful in judging the size of your design.

03 | Roll and texture fresh clay 2 to 4 cards thick. Use the paper patterns for templates as you cut the pieces of the building. Embellish the strips of clay while they're fresh, including windows

IDEA | TURRETS

If you want to make a turret ring, form the building out of a single sheet and let it dry in the round around a dowel or other suitable form.

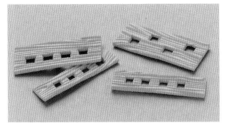

The four sides of a woody Tree Building, ready to assemble.

Box sides, attached one at a time. I often wait to cut my base and roof until I have assembled the body of my buildings.

if you like. Use a sharp tissue blade or very clean cutters to cut out your pieces. Heal the cuts after they're made by gently stroking them with your fingertip to avoid unnecessary filing or sanding later.

04 | Lay the pieces flat and allow them to become hard leather-hard to bone-dry.

05 | Use a wash of water on each piece to be joined to squidge the strips of dry clay together into a building form. Let the building dry completely. You may find it easiest to let each side dry after it's attached so that you don't accidentally dislodge previous sides when attaching new ones.

06 | Use a wash of water to squidge the bottom of the building to the dry ring top pad. Add a roof if desired.

Let the whole piece dry, then fully fire, either upside down on a shelf if you have a flat roof, or nestled in a dish of vermiculite.

07 | Use a hammer and ring mandrel to work-harden the ring band. Tumble, brush, and patina the piece as desired, finishing to taste.

Work-hardening the ring shank against an anvil.

IDEA | WAVE FRONT RING

Yet another way to make a building ring: the simple **WAVE FRONT RING.** To do so, curve a flat sheet of rolled and textured clay into a modern building form. Let it dry and attach the dried, curved building to the pad with the embedded strap band.

amphora
pendant

One of my favorite fictional characters, Hercule Poirot, always wore a silver boutonniere on his vest, given to him as a young man by one of the two women he ever loved. Make this interesting amphora setting to show off a favorite bead; to practice your appliqué, fusing, chain-making, and open box-building skills; and to evoke the well-dressed Poirot and his romantic devotion.

FINISHED SIZE

necklace 22¼" (56.5 cm)
pendant 1¼" x 2¾" x ½"
(3.2 x 7 x 1.3 cm)

MATERIALS

50–75 g of fine silver clay for Amphora

50–75 g of fine silver clay for chain (optional)

1 glass 14x63mm tube bead or size of choice

1" (2.5 cm) of 10– or 12–gauge fine silver wire to snugly fit bead hole

16 or more dry fine silver clay 8mm rings

12 or more dry fine silver clay 3mm balls

2 fine silver 15mm jump rings + 2 fine silver 13x30mm S-clasps or 8" (20.3 cm) of 12-gauge fine silver wire

Liver of sulfur

2-part epoxy resin

TOOLS

Work surface

Roller

Rolling guides

Texture pads or rubber stamps

Sharp tissue blade

Heavy-duty flush cutters

Soft paintbrush + water

Cocktail straw or small drill bit + drill

³⁄₁₆" (5 mm) circle cutter

Ball-end burnisher

Kiln

Hammer

Anvil

Tumbler

Flat- or chain-nose pliers

Torch (optional)

Kiln brick (optional)

Large round-nose pliers (optional)

Brass brush

Lampworked bead by Stephanie Sersich

amphora necklace

PROJECT NOTES

This lovely project can be made entirely of metal clay. Just create larger hanging holes and attach a metal clay chain directly to the pendant. I used S-hooks to connect my piece so the chain could be removable, giving the option of wearing the amphora on a plain, less expensive chain if desired.

TECHNIQUES + ELEMENTS

Box-building (page 60)
Simple rivet posts (page 50)
Appliqué (page 24)
Rings (page 36)
Metal clay chain (page 73)
S-clasp (page 46)
Fused wire chain (page 69) (optional)

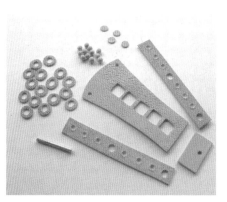

The parts to the Amphora, bone-dry and ready to assemble. Note the pilot hole I made in the pad, using the piece of 10-gauge wire that will eventually be embedded. The pilot hole will shrink just a bit as the base dries, making it nice and grabby when the wire is finally inserted prior to firing.

01 | BACK. Roll and texture a sheet of fresh metal clay to a finished thickness of 3–4 cards. Cut an elongated fan shape, $1\frac{5}{8}$" × $3\frac{1}{8}$" (4.1 × 8 cm), to form the amphora's back. Cut decorative windows in the back of the piece, to show the bead from behind and to cut the weight of your finished piece. Cut hanging holes at the top right and left corners, either when the clay is bone-dry, using a small drill bit, or when it is fresh, using a cocktail straw. If you cut fresh, you can remove the cut material from your cocktail straw, and either use it to roll a little ball of clay for an egg (page 20) or a ball-end head pin (page 40). Let the back

piece become hard leather-hard to bone-dry, and, if you wish, appliqué small pieces of dry clay to it for interest. I used three plain circles, cut from a thinly rolled sheet with a drinking straw, and attached them bone-dry, with a wash of water. **NOTE** *I used a long, narrow lampworked bead for my design, but you can use any large bead for yours; just design the setting to accommodate the bead size.*

02 | SIDE RECTANGLES. Roll and texture a sheet of fresh metal clay to a finished thickness of 3–4 cards. Cut two $\frac{1}{2}$" × 3" (1.3 × 7.6 cm) rectangles. Use a ball-end burnisher to make small divots along the length of the rectangles where you'll add the dry clay rings. Use the circle cutter to cut out a few of the divots; the rings will frame the holes later. Let the rectangles become hard leather-hard to bone-dry.

It can be helpful to lay your 8mm bone-dry clay rings onto the freshly cut sides, to help you position your divots.

03 | BASE. Roll a plain sheet of fresh metal clay 6 cards thick. Cut a ⅝" × 1" (1.5 × 2.5 cm) rectangle to form the amphora's base. Use the wire that will support the bead to make a hole in the base where a rivet post will go. Keep in mind that the hole may not be dead center, depending on the fit of your bead in your setting. Let the base become hard leather-hard to bone-dry. **NOTE** *This rivet post will hold your bead in place, so be sure to choose a wire gauge that fits your bead hole tightly. Beware of large beads with tiny holes; you want your wire to be thick enough to support the weight of the bead without bending.*

Place the dry clay balls in the drop of water in your dry clay divots, and let them get sticky.

04 | Use water and pressure to squidge the dry clay rings to the two dry ½" × 3" (1.3 × 7.6 cm) rectangles so they frame the divots or cut-out holes. For the rings that frame a divot, fill the ring with a drop of water and drop in 1 dry clay ball.

Let the balls set up briefly, and, when sticky, press and rotate them in their divots to secure.

05 | Use a small amount of water and pressure to squidge the box sides together, assembling an open box form. Brush the joins with a damp paintbrush to gently smooth and clean them.

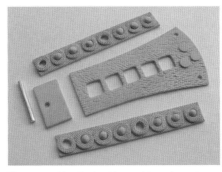

The prepared box back, sides, and base, bone-dry and ready for assembly.

06 | Let the box dry completely. Fill any errors in your joinery, if necessary, with tiny snakes of freshly rolled clay, and smooth in place with a thin wash of water or slip. Let the box completely dry.

07 | OPTIONAL. Make and assemble a 16" to 24" (41 to 61 cm) metal clay chain for hanging the pendant (see *Metal clay chain*, page 73.)

The finished box form, ready for the post embed and firing, and a finished Amphora box in the background. Note the different look of flush vs. high sides.

08 | Reset the rivet post into the hole in your base, which should have shrunk in drying. This is one of my favorite techniques to get a really good fit on a large wire embed; make the hole in wet clay, and set the post in the dry clay. The drying process offers just enough shrinkage to ensure a tight fit of the wire in the hole. Fire the box and chain for 2 hours at 1650° F (899° C).

09 | After firing, work-harden the chain by hammering the links on the anvil and a bezel mandrel.

10 | Attach one commercial or hand-made fine silver jump ring to each of the hanging holes. Fuse the rings closed if desired.

bird on a branch necklace

This lovely design marries the sculptural beauty and texture of metal clay with the solidity and strength of fine silver wire. Covering a wire armature with metal clay can act as a springboard for many other designs; almost anything you can think of that can be built as a wire armature can be covered in metal clay and fired.

FINISHED SIZE
3" x 2½" x ¾"
(7.6 x 6.4 x 1.9 cm)

MATERIALS

10–25 g fine silver metal clay
1½" (3.8 cm) of 18-gauge fine silver wire
12" (30.5 cm) of 14- or 16-gauge fine silver wire
3"–6" (7.6–15.2 cm) of 12-gauge fine silver wire
1 fine silver 15mm jump ring
2 fine silver 20mm jump rings
1 glass, metal, or resin 1" (2.5 cm) bird bead
2-part epoxy resin
Any length of chain suitable for a necklace
Clasp (optional)

TOOLS

Working surface
Sharp tissue blade
Measuring spoon or dapping block
Cocktail straw
Flush cutters
1½" (3.8 cm) flower-shaped cookie cutter (optional)
Soft paintbrush and water
Dapping block or small round ball
Vermiculite + firing dish (optional)
Kiln
Brass brush
Drinking straw
Round-nose pliers
Hammer
Anvil
Metal hole punch
Bead awl
Liver of sulfur (optional)
Tumbler (optional)
Buffing papers, polishing cloth (optional)
Torch (optional)
Kiln brick (optional)
Flat-nose pliers

Lampworked bead by Kim Fields

bird on a branch necklace

PROJECT NOTES

This charming piece is simple to make. Any type of ornament will work, and the branch bar, if pierced on the ends, can easily be connected to any type of chain with sturdy jump rings. I chose to rivet my eggs and nest onto the branch with the help of two rivet posts at the top of the armature. I added a balled and pierced wire at the branch's bottom so I could hang a set of fine silver flowers from it. For my chain, I chose to fuse fine silver rings, each one about 1/2" (1.3 cm) in diameter.

I strongly recommend fine silver wire instead of sterling for your support wire. If you use sterling, admittedly you will gain strength in your wire, but you'll have to underfire your metal clay piece, which I don't think is worth the tradeoff. If you use 14- or 12-gauge fine silver wire for your branch armature, it will be plenty of support for your sculpture.

TECHNIQUES + ELEMENTS

Branches (page 48)
Egg clutch (page 128)
Fused wire chain (page 69)

The little glass owl bead and the finished nest and egg clutch, awaiting assembly.

01 | NEST. Sculpt a 1/2"–1" (1.3–2.5 cm) wide stick nest out of layers of tiny, rolled metal clay snakes, cut into short lengths, woven together, and set over an upside down measuring spoon or inside a divot in a dapping block. Use a cocktail straw to cut a hole in the center of the nest, if necessary, and let it dry completely. Nestle the nest in a small dish of vermiculite and set aside for firing. **NOTE** *You'll fire this piece in the desired curvature, rather than firing it*

The patinated stick nest was made by weaving many little rolled cylinders together and letting them dry over a rounded form. I used a measuring spoon.

flat and dapping it, so you don't flatten the delicate detailing.

02 | BRANCH BAR. Use the 12-gauge wire to form a 3"–5" (7.6–12.7 cm) base branch. Use 16- or 14-gauge wire to wrap additional twigs or branchlets around the base, keeping in mind that you'll need to leave enough wire sticking up to use as a rivet or epoxy post for your

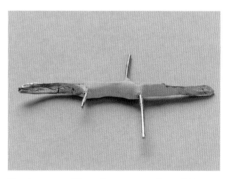

The clay-covered branch armature, prior to firing.

ornaments. If you plan on riveting, use 14-gauge wire, or step up to 12-gauge if your ornaments are large or heavy. Cover the finished armature with metal clay as described on page 48, leaving enough bare wire sticking out for your rivets or glue posts. Spear a 1/16"–1/4" (2–6 mm) ball of metal clay on each end of the bar. Make your decision

TIP | BIRD SCULPTING

You can easily craft your own metal clay bird for this project. If your bird has a neck, you might want to sculpt the head and body separately, and attach the two together with a small piece of 18-gauge fine silver wire. This is a sculptural technique often used in traditional clay work. Make a hole halfway through the center of the body if you plan to attach the bird to the branch with resin; make it all the way through for attaching it with a rivet or a wire wrap.

about ball size based on the weight of the chain and the delicacy of your piece. Keep in mind that the ball will be hammered and flattened, then pierced. If you've added a bottom twig for hanging flowers or other ornaments, as I did, spear that wire with a small rolled ball of metal clay as well. Be certain not to handle or disrupt the balls of clay after they are attached; like embeds, they need to dry tightly in place. Let the branch bar dry completely, and set aside for firing. The bar can fire flat on a kiln shelf, or, if you have a lot of different angles and protrusions, in a shallow dish, nestled in vermiculite.

IDEA | DIFFERENT BIRD DIFFERENT LOOK

I also placed Karen Elmquist's **PEEVISH HEAD** owl on my branch bar to see what I thought of him for this design, but decided to finish the piece with a little white owl from Kim Fields. If you use a bird other than an owl or raptor, you may wish to modify your nest and eggs to reflect the correct size, shape, and texture for the species.

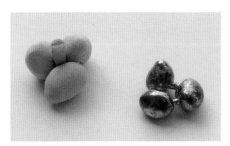

Place a toothpick section in the middle of your EGG CLUTCH to preserve space for the rivet post.

03 | EGG CLUTCH. Form 3 freshly rolled ³⁄₁₆"–¹⁄₄" (4 to 6 mm) metal clay eggs. Attach them into a triad with three small cuts of 18-gauge wire. If you choose to use only one egg for your nest, make a hole all the way through it, so it can sit beneath the bird or on the rivet post. Set the egg clutch aside for firing. **NOTE** *If the space in the center of your egg clutch is very small, place a section of a toothpick in the center hole to preserve the hole during firing.*

04 | FLOWERS. If you wish, sculpt three flowers of any size that include hanging loops as in *Circlet of Flowers Necklace* (page 105): Roll a lightly textured sheet of fresh clay 2–3 cards thick. Use the cookie cutter to cut 3

Three fine silver flowers caught on a fused fine silver wire ring and hanging from the bottom wire of the branch, which was balled, hammered, and pierced after firing.

flower shapes, smooth the edges, and allow them to dry in a dap cup or over a small round ball. Cut bail strips for the flowers out of 2-card-thick fresh clay. Allow the strips to dry over a drinking straw. Once the flowers and strips are hard leather-hard or bone-dry, add a wash of water to the strip ends and use some delicate, yet firm, squidging to attach it to the back of the flower. Let

dry and set aside for firing. Make two extra flowers, if you like, for a pair of matching earrings.

05 | Fully fire the nest, branch bar, egg clutch, flowers, and, if you sculpted your own, the bird. Hammer the balls at the end of the branch bar flat, and pierce them with a drill or hole punch. Do the same for the bottom hanging twig if you're attaching ornaments. Clean and/or open up the punched holes with a bead awl.

06 | If desired, cut the chain into two equal segments and add one half of the clasp to one end of each chain. **NOTE** *I used handmade fine silver fused chain (page 69) but this piece looks beautiful with many different types of chain. I particularly love the look of two or three strands of vintage brass chain used together.*

07 | Use one 20mm jump ring to connect each loose chain end an end loop on the branch bar. Fuse or solder the rings closed if desired.

08 | Clean, brush, patina, and tumble the branch bar and chain, nest, egg clutch, flowers, and bird to taste.

09 | Wire wrap, rivet, or epoxy the bird, nest, and egg clutch to the branch bar.

10 | Slide the flowers onto the 15mm jump ring and add it to the center hanging post; fuse or solder the ring closed if desired. Brush and add finish with patina or a polishing cloth to taste.

terms

The technical and project-based lingo used by metalsmiths and metal clay artisans is fairly straightforward, but there are a few technical terms that are helpful to fully understand. I've separated this section into clay and metalsmithing terms because you'll need an understanding of each set of processes to take advantage of the full potential of metal clay, and, in some cases, to see that what we don't have to do (fluxing our metal before flame-joining, for example) is as important as what we will do.

Clay Terms

APPLIQUÉ. The joining of one piece of clay to another, usually when both pieces have a flat side. This technique is usually used for surface decoration. Appliqué also correctly describes the process of some structural joins, when adhering one flat surface to the other with the aid of water or slip (page 132).

BONE-DRY. Completely dry clay. When the clay has moisture inside it evaporating out, the surface will feel cool or cold. You can judge the ambient humidity of a room, which defines how long you have to work your clay, by how cool the clay feels as it starts to dry. If it feels very cold as it dries, you are in a dry environ-ment and evaporation is happening quickly. If this is the case, you have very little work time. Slightly cool? Evaporation is happening more slowly, and your environment is likely more humid. In a humid environment, you have more time to play with shape and texture. Use a room humidifier, or dehumidifier, if you'd like to adjust your working time. Bone-dry clay will feel room temperature, not cooler.

FIRING. Heating your metal clay pieces to burn out the binders and sinter them together (see **FIRING**, page 25).

GREENWARE. Dry, unfired clay pieces. Greenware can wait forever on a shelf until you are ready to fire it, so if you don't have a kiln, you

The **RETURNING RING** (above + page 109) takes advantage of both clay and metalsmithing techniques. Below, a fired **FIRST KISS PIPE RING** and a greenware version, ready for the kiln.

terms

might want to save up your greenware pieces, then pay a studio to fire them for you. Keep in mind that if you want a full two-hour, 1650° F (899° C) firing, you need to ask for it, because (sadly) many studios do not fully fire their metal clay.

HAND-BUILDING. A way of making objects out of clay that doesn't use a potter's wheel. Hand-builders work primarily with slabs, coils, and balls of clay. Hand-building techniques learned with traditional clay transfer quite well to metal clay, although in most cases, you'll be working in a smaller format. You won't need a large mechanical slab roller, for example, just a little tube of PVC and a few small rolling guides. The best advice I give people coming over from a regular clay background is to back off on the water and slip, don't score your attachment points, and don't ever stretch or pull metal clay. If you stretch it, you create molecularly thin and weak areas in your finished metal. Also, leather-hard or bone-dry metal clay is quite willing to join to its neighboring pieces without any scoring, as long as the joints you make are clean, neat, and smooth. Any book on clay hand-building will be very helpful to your metal clay work, as long as you remember those caveats.

LEATHER-HARD + HARD LEATHER-HARD. These terms describe the amount of moisture remaining in the clay. When clay is fresh, it's described as fresh, wet, or soft. When the surface begins to dry, the interior of the piece will still be moist. Leather-hard clay literally feels like a piece of leather; the surface is cool and you can tell by holding it that it could still be flexed or bent. Hard leather-hard describes a state where there is still moisture at the center of the piece, but the dryness has reached a point at which flexing the clay would break it. If you like to carve clay, you'll want to do it while it's in the territory between leather-hard and hard leather-hard. You'll know that your clay is at the right place for carving when you push your carving tool along the piece and it pulls up a lovely little curl with slightly cracked edges and leaves behind a smooth channel. Clay pieces of any kind are defined by their moments, and choosing the right moment to work a piece will mean the difference between easy success and a difficult battle. Unlike traditional clay bodies like porcelain or terra cotta, the perfect moment to work your metal clay may pass and can't be regained. So it pays to be mindful and work on very few pieces at a time.

SHORT-FIRING + UNDERFIRING. Firing your pieces for either too little time, at too low of a temperature, or both. The firing directions in the packets of metal clay could lead one to believe that short firings or underfirings are acceptable, but they aren't if you want to make structurally sound work.

SLIP. Slip is a slurry of dry clay and water and is, by nature, less dense than the metal clay out of the package.

SLIP JOINT. The area where two metal clay pieces are joined with slip. Slip joints have fewer metal particles and are more likely to break under the stress of drilling, hammering, or sawing. When possible, make joins with only a small amount of water, and use pressure and the natural stickiness of wetted bone-dry clay to make your connections. Filling gaps with slip is asking for weak spots in your work and is not recommended for structural joins like that of ring bands or pendant bails. Fill gaps instead with thinly rolled snakes of fresh clay (page 22), worked in with a bit of water or slip.

SQUIDGING. To use pressure and movement to bond two pieces of unfired metal clay together, using water or slip as the bonding agent.

WET CLAY. You'd think this meant wet with water, but not really. It just means fresh, soft, and pliable—right out of the package. Water-wet clay isn't something that you really want, unless you are in a traditional clay studio. Some people choose to add water to their fresh metal clay, almost always with bad result. The best way to add moisture to metal clay is to place it in a small, airtight container with a drop of water smeared on the inside lid. Let the container of clay sit overnight, and it will have absorbed the drop. Alternatively, you can roll your too-dry bit of metal clay in with fresh clay, and let them sit together in an airtight plastic container overnight. Don't include more than 10% dry clay to 90% fresh for best results.

Metalsmithing Terms

ALLOY. An alloy is a mixture of two or more elements, of which one or more is a metal. Alloying is commonly done to increase the hardness, strength, ductility, luster, or tarnish resistance of the resulting product. Sterling silver is an alloy of 92.5% fine silver, and 7.5% other materials. Copper is usually the dominant portion of the 7.5%, but nickel, zinc, germanium, and other metals and additives, including silicon and boron, could be mixed in. Different alloys have different properties, and alloys are generally chosen by metalsmiths with an eye to the finished product. Some alloys are more suitable for casting; some are engineered for strength, durability of finish, or tarnish resistance. Lower quality sterling silver will generally be short on copper and long on nickel or zinc.

ANNEALING. This process brings a material to a temperature at which its grains coalesce and smooth. The material assumes its natural molecular form and pattern or makes progress toward its equilibrium state. For example, an-nealing glass beads (assuming that the beads were made with compatible glasses) turns a lot of stuck-together parts like dots and stringer into one solid mass of glass and eliminates points of stress. Annealing metal does much the same thing; it provides a slow heat soak, which allows diffusion of atoms, reducing dislocations, smoothing imperfect grain boundaries, and relieving internal stresses. This process also renders the material dead soft. Dead soft metal must be work-hardened before it's ready for duty.

A full two-hour firing of your metal clay pieces will not only fully sinter your work, but will provide a long enough annealing soak for the piece to refine molecularly. Stresses dissolve, fractures disappear, and gradually the

THE BIRD ON A BRANCH not only shows off many sculptural clay techniques, such as a stick nest made of rolled snakes of clay, a covered wire armature, and a handmade metal clay chain, but it also takes advantage of several mechanical metalsmithing techniques, such as hammered and pierced ball ends and a rivet.

terms

number of grains decreases. Technically, sintering may be complete after only ten minutes at 1650° F (899° C), but the piece won't be fully annealed. A piece that has not been fully de-stressed by annealing after sintering will have higher porosity, more fracture lines and break points, and generally will not hold up to forming, hammering, drilling, sawing, or hard wear.

BAIL. A loop, ring, or section of tube that allows a piece to be hung from a chain or wire. I make most of my bails with imbedded fine silver wire.

BEZEL. A setting that encircles a stone or ornament and holds it in place. I often form my bezels with flat fine silver bezel wire, but they can really be made of anything that can be formed around an object.

CASTING. This technique involves pouring a liquid material into a mold and allowing it to solidify into the shape of that mold. Casting is a great way to make multiples of pieces, whether for mass production, or just to make a series of a favorite piece. Metal clay is perfect for making casting models, and can also be melted, along with fine silver wire scrap, into pure fine silver, and used to pour into molds, or to cast ingots for rolling sheet or drawing wire. Most home studios aren't set up for casting because production casting involves using quantities of molten metal, which is dangerous. The technique also requires fairly expensive equipment, such as vacuum chambers and centrifuges. However, simple sand or single mold casting can be done with a small pouring crucible of melted scrap, and small ingots can be cast in the same way. This book doesn't deal with the casting process, but there are many that do, if you're interested in learning. Fine silver, being a pure metal, is quite simple to melt and cast with. Melting and casting alloys, such as sterling silver, is considerably more complex. Even if you don't cast in your own studio, you can use metal clay to make original casting models, which you can send to a casting studio to reproduce in any quantity. Most casting models are sculpted in wax and are lost in the mold-making process, but a model crafted in metal clay will be a solid fine silver object, undamaged by the process of reproduction. It's nice to have the original of a series; metal clay makes this possible.

COLD JOIN. A mechanical connection that doesn't rely on heat. Examples of cold joins are rivets, staples, and jump rings.

DAP. To hammer a piece of flat metal into a curved or domed shape.

DEAD SOFT. Metal's post-annealing state. Dead soft metal has few internal stresses or deformities and is soft and easy to bend or work. You can achieve a dead soft state with your fired metal clay by annealing it with a torch or in a kiln. Annealing can be done as frequently as and at any time you wish, provided your piece does not have resin, glass, gemstones, or other flammable embellishments installed. Keep in mind that firing metal clay also anneals it, and all pieces will come out of the kiln dead soft. If you've ordered wire or sheet metal dead soft, it means it has been annealed after it was drawn, rolled, or formed.

FINE SILVER. Pure fine silver is 99.9% pure silver, also known as "three nines fine." Fine silver offers a huge advantage in that it can be fused without solder or flux, and does not discolor or firescale when heated. Fine silver will come away from heat with a layer of white silver oxide on its surface, which can be brushed off with a brass brush or patinated.

FIRESCALE. A stain below the surface of metal, resulting from overheating and oxidation of the copper in sterling silver. Firescale will not appear on fine silver, nor will tarnish, as it has no copper added.

FORGING. Hammering a piece to spread and shape it, usually with the periodic application of heat to anneal as the metal stiffens. Some metal is forged hot, like iron, but fine silver is forged cold. I often forge my chain links, ring shanks, and the simple loops of my heavy-gauge head pins (page 44). To do so, use heavy-duty round-nose pliers to form a simple loop at the end of the head pin, then hammer the loop with a stroking motion until it spreads and flattens. Forging makes metal very hard and functional.

FLUX. A chemical compound used in soldering. It is commonly used to prevent the oxidation of the copper in sterling silver because solder doesn't stick well to the oxides that copper forms when heated. Flux also improves the flow of solder, making the join happen more quickly and more cleanly than it would without flux. Most flux produces toxic vapors when heated and should only be used with professional ventilation.

FUSING. Melting particles together. For metal clay, it refers to joining fine silver pieces without solder, by heating the metal until it flows. I do my fusing with a small jeweler's torch or with a hand-held professional butane torch.

FUSING TEMPERATURE. The temperature at which the grains of a material soften and begin to melt together. The fusing temperature of fine silver begins at approximately 1700° F (927° C), and the metal will begin to melt and flow at approximately 1761° F (961° C). The suggested firing temperature for fine silver metal clay is 1650° F (899° C), which approaches the fusing temperature as closely as possible, but does not risk losing the surface texture and detail through melting or slumping in the kiln. The closer you come to fusing temperature, the better your particles of metal will be bonded together after sintering.

GAUGE. Wire is measured in gauges, with the largest numbers representing the thinnest wires. When adding wire to my metal clay pieces I generally use 18-, 16-, and 14-gauge fine silver wire, especially for my head pin and charm imbeds. For making ring shanks, I usually use 12- or 10-gauge; for making chain, I use 14- or 12-gauge. Anything finer than

18-gauge is too soft to be useful in fine silver and anything over 12-gauge is very difficult to bend.

PATINA. The color or stain on a surface. Metal can be stained with a wide variety of chemicals, some more toxic than others. I use liver of sulfur because it's the safest both to use and dispose of, and it gives a wide range of color. You can also achieve fabulous color on metal with pigment pencils, plant stains, paints, etc., but these surfaces require sealing. Patina can be left unsealed or can be sealed (temporarily) with spray-on sealers or hard waxes. Unsealed patina will continue to evolve, requiring a collaboration with the owner of the piece, either to keep the piece polished, periodically restore the patina, or let the piece evolve naturally. Of course, sealing a patina is only a temporary maneuver; the wax or spray will eventually wear off, leaving the wearer with exactly the same choices.

PICKLE. The charming word deployed by metalsmiths to describe a usually toxic, steaming brew of sulfuric, hydrochloric, or nitric acid, alone or in combination. Pickle is used to remove impurities, stains, rust, or scale from metals. It is what most smiths use to clean sterling silver after soldering or heating.

terms

Happily, fine silver does not stain, scale, or blacken when heated, so unless you are using sterling silver or other alloys in your work, you can skip the steaming Crock-Pot-of-Doom. Pickle, obviously, should only be used in a well-ventilated room. Some new pickles have come on the market that are citrus-based and marketed as nontoxic; they may work more slowly or less thoroughly, but are probably a good compromise for people who need to clean sterling but don't want to breathe sulfuric or nitric acid fumes.

QUENCH. To quickly cool molten or very hot metal in water.

RIVET. A cold join made by placing a piece of wire through corresponding holes in two or more pieces then flaring or doming the ends of the wire to be larger than the holes, trapping the objects on the wire. Rivet posts can be set into fresh metal clay and then dried and fired in place for a very easy rivet. Alternatively, a free rivet can be formed by balling and flattening one end of a piece of wire and using that flattened end as the rivet base (page 78).

SILVER FUMING. The process of catching a stream of vaporized silver on an object. Glass beadmakers frequently do this in the flame of their torch. It leaves a fine film of silver on the surface of the glass and vaporized silver in your breathing space. Don't ever do this without professional fume ventilation. Firing metal clay poses no risk of silver fuming, unless the kiln drastically overfires and melts the metal. When fusing fine silver, the surface flows, resulting in a small amount of vaporization. Fusing should always be done with a fresh air supply, ideally with a vent hood, unless only a few pieces are being fused. Wearing masks or respirators is only effective while the masks are on; if you are creating pollution in your studio airspace, wearing a mask may not fully protect you from dust or fumes that linger after the event.

SINTERING. The process of using heat or pressure, or both, to join small particles or powders until they adhere into a whole. In the final stages of a full metal clay firing, the annealing process allows the already sintered metal atoms to move, smoothing and eliminating grain boundaries and filling molecular gaps. Poorly sintered and annealed work shrinks a bit less and breaks more easily, as

you well know if you've handled underfired metal clay pieces. Happily, poorly fired metal clay can be refired fully as long as it contains no inclusions (like glass) that can't take the heat of a full firing.

SOLDER. Base metal paste, sheet, or wire used to join two pieces of metal. Solder flows at a lower temperature than the metal being joined, and comes in various formulas designed to melt at different temperatures.

SOLDERING. Joining metal with solder. Soldering works best if you use flux to prepare the surface. Most solder and flux, even those touted as "green," release toxic fumes when heated. Soldering should only be done with professional ventilation. I usually carry my solder tray outside, if possible, and do the work in the fresh air. Because fine silver can be joined without the use of solder or flux, it's a safe choice for someone who wants to run a clean shop but still make hot connections in metal. I sometimes choose to "sweat solder" my metal clay pieces together. Sweat soldering involves placing solder between two flat pieces of metal and heating the piece so that the solder flows between the flat pieces. This can be a very effective way to build rings.

If you choose to use solder with metal clay, it will help to burnish the surface first to diminish the porosity of the metal.

STERLING SILVER. Sterling silver is an alloy of fine silver and copper with other metals or additives sometimes mixed in (see **ALLOY**, page 133) to make it stronger and longer-wearing than fine silver. Sterling silver begins to break down at temperatures over 1500° F (816° C), so should not be fired at 1650° F (899° C). Sterling silver blackens and can firescale when heated. It requires solder and flux to join it, because the temperatures required to fuse or flow the metal will break down the alloy. This blackening requires an acid soak and/or aggressive buffing to clean. The advantage to imbedding sterling silver additions like wire or jump rings into your metal clay work is that they are stronger and often come in smaller gauges than fine silver, but that one advantage may not be worth the compromise you make for the structural integrity of the metal clay when required to fire it at a lower temperature. I personally only use fine silver imbeds in my fine silver metal clay, because I want to fire all of my work fully.

TARNISH. Tarnish is a layer of grimy corrosion that forms over metals, such as sterling silver, that contain copper, aluminum, or other metals that react chemically with their environment. Oxygen and sulfur are the two main chemical triggers of tarnish on silver. Tarnish is a surface effect and can easily be cleaned from the metal with a polishing cloth. Tarnish is generally regarded as "dirty," while patina is thought of as a decorative finish, although both are technically just oxidation effects. Fine silver will not technically "tarnish" because it contains no copper, but it will accept patina, as the fine silver oxides will react with sulfur or other chemicals and compounds.

WORK-HARDENING. The process of disrupting the annealed state. Hitting the metal with hammers or mallets deforms the metal grains and disrupts the structure of the metal to create moderate internal stresses, which results in increased stiffness. Continuing to work or bend a piece of metal after work-hardening can result in breakage. Anneal a work-hardened piece of metal at any time during the forming process to return it to a dead soft state. If you've ever watched a blacksmith work, you've seen this process in action; heating, forming, then stiffness setting into the metal, and then back to the furnace to heat the piece again so that the smith can continue forming. If your own metalwork becomes stiff from overworking, you can anneal it (page 133) at any time to start over from dead soft.

Tumblers can be used for light-duty work-hardening, but almost all fine silver jewelry pieces can benefit from more aggressive work-hardening. Think of a tumbler full of stainless steel shot as a chamber of a thousand mosquitoes with hammers—useful to a point, but perhaps insufficient for the end goal.

resources

General Supplies

Check your local jewelry-making, bead, and craft shops for supplies or contact these online vendors:

RIO GRANDE

7500 Bluewater Rd., NW
Albuquerque, NM 87121
(800) 545-6566
riogrande.com

Rio Grande offers volume discounts on PMC and fine silver wire, and is the exclusive vendor for Swanstrom pliers. I use 6" flat-, round-nose, and heavy-duty round-nose Swanstrom pliers daily. Rio also sells the Eurotool flush cutter I prefer, plus an assortment of Wrap and Tap tools, professional ring and bezel mandrels, anvils, blocks, dap sets, PMC kilns, and an assortment of fine silver and gold findings, gems, and synthetic stones that can be imbedded into metal clay.

METAL CLAY FINDINGS

49 Hurdis St.
North Providence, RI 02904
(888) 999-6404
metalclayfindings.com

The good people at Metal Clay Findings are always looking for the next great idea. They have a beautiful selection of components and parts to make your designs go smoothly.

COOL TOOLS

(888) 478-5060
cooltools.us

Cool Tools has a stunning selection of texture sheets and about every tool or gadget on the market for metal clay. Cool Tools also sells metal clay, kilns, and has a great selection of books, thin medical tissue blades, round-end burnishers, rolling guides, and hand tools.

KEMPER TOOLS

kempertools.com

Kemper makes handy cutter sets for clay. I have them all. The company also makes my favorite round-end burnishers and have a wealth of traditional clay tools. Kemper doesn't sell retail, but they can point you to a supplier in your area.

FUSION BEADS
(888) 781-3559
fusionbeads.com

The nice beadists at Fusion Beads sell my favorite two-hole metal punch. They have a nice selection of Wrap + Taps—which they call coiling pliers—and other tools as well. And beads! TONS of beads!

ARROW SPRINGS
4301 A Product Dr.
Shingle Springs, CA 95682
(800) 899-0689
arrowsprings.com

Get your kiln bricks for fusing, and possibly your kiln, from Arrow Springs. If you are in the market for a kiln that can serve multiple functions in your studio, the knowledgeable people at Arrow Springs will help you choose the right one or build one to your specifications.

HARBOR FREIGHT TOOLS
harborfreight.com

Harbor Freight carries my favorite inexpensive rock tumbler. Not only is it cheap, but it has an on/off switch. It's a pity that that a power switch is a rare feature in a tumbler, because we're almost always using them with wet hands and don't want to be plugging and unplugging to turn our tumblers on and off. Tumbler belts break on a regular basis, but can easily be replaced with sturdy rubber bands for a quick interim fix. I also buy rough hammers and anvils from Harbor Freight, which often has great deals on inexpensive vises, blocks, and other bench tools. Don't expect precision or fine crafting; go to a jeweler's supply house, like Rio Grande, for that. Harbor Freight has locations everywhere; check the site to see if there is one near you.

Beadmakers

Kim Fields
Northfire Designs
3593 Timber Ridge Dr.
Metamora, MI 48455
(810) 678-3896
northfiredesigns.com

Amy Johnson
TANK fire + metal
Studio 105, Bldg. 74,
Distillery District
Toronto, Canada
(647) 430-8589
tankstudio.com

Stephanie Sersich
SSS Beads
15 Perkins St.
Topsham, ME 04086
(207) 373-1654
sssbeads.com

Dustin Tabor
dustintabor.com

Karen Elmquist
karenelmquist.com

Joyce Rooks
Torchsong
joycerooks.com

about
the author

KATE MCKINNON is a mixed-media artist who lives and works in Tucson, Arizona. Her work focuses on the engineering of how elements work together, connect, and grow into finished pieces of jewelry. She has made a life study of small tasks, always asking, "How could this be better, stronger, simpler, or more elegant?"

Kate started working in metal clay when it was first introduced in America, and her work stands out in her field for its focus, not only on professional construction, but also on safe handling. She won the prestigious Rio Grande Saul Bell award in 2005 for her innovative design with the product, and she has taught and lectured internationally.

index

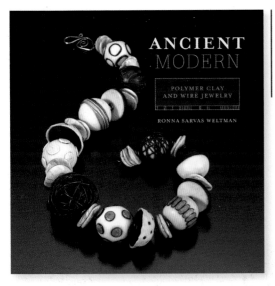